HOW TO
Support
Struggling Students

ROBYN R. JACKSON | CLAIRE LAMBERT

ASCD

Alexandria, Virginia USA

mindsteps

Washington, DC

1703 N. Beauregard St. • Alexandria, VA 22311-1714 USA
Phone: 800-933-2723 or 703-578-9600 • Fax: 703-575-5400
Web site: www.ascd.org • E-mail: member@ascd.org
Author guidelines: www.ascd.org/write

mindsteps™
Washington, DC
Phone: 888-565-8881
Web site: www.mindstepsinc.com

Gene R. Carter, *Executive Director;* Judy Zimny, *Chief Program Development Officer,* Nancy Modrak, *Publisher;* Scott Willis, *Director, Book Acquisitions & Development;* Genny Ostertag, *Acquisitions Editor;* Julie Houtz, *Director, Book Editing & Production;* Katie Martin, *Editor;* Reece Quiñones, *Senior Graphic Designer;* Mike Kalyan, *Production Manager;* Keith Demmons, *Desktop Publishing Specialist*

All Web links in this book are correct as of the publication date below but may have become inactive or otherwise modified since that time. If you notice a deactivated or changed link, please e-mail books@ascd.org with the words "Link Update" in the subject line. In your message, please specify the Web link, the book title, and the page number on which the link appears.

PAPERBACK ISBN: 978-1-4166-1084-7   ASCD product #110073   n7/20

Quantity discounts for the paperback edition only: 10–49 copies, 10%; 50+ copies, 15%; for 1,000 or more copies, call 800-933-2723, ext. 5634, or 703-575-5634. For desk copies: member@ascd.org.

Library of Congress Cataloging-in-Publication Data

Jackson, Robyn Renee.
  How to support struggling students / Robyn R. Jackson, Claire Lambert.
      p. cm. – (Mastering the principles of great teaching series)
  Includes bibliographical references and index.
  ISBN 978-1-4166-1084-7 (pbk. : alk. paper) 1. School improvement programs–United States. 2. Underachievers–Education (Secondary)–United States. 3. Learning strategies–United States. I. Lambert, Claire M. II. Title.
  LB2822.82.J27 2010
  371.93–dc22

20 19 18 17 16 15 14 13 12 11 10   1 2 3 4 5 6 7 8 9 10 11 12

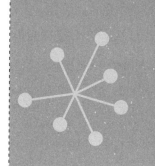

MASTERING
THE PRINCIPLES OF GREAT
TEACHING

How to Support Struggling Students

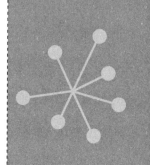

About the Mastering the Principles of Great Teaching Series

Have you ever wondered what it takes to become a master teacher? Sure, you know what master teachers do—what their classrooms look like, how they structure their lessons, the kinds of assessments they give, and the strategies they use. But becoming a master teacher involves more than simply doing what master teachers do. To be a master teacher, you need to *think* like a master teacher.

If you ask master teachers their secret, they may not be able to tell you. That's because most master teachers have a difficult time explaining what makes them masterful in the classroom. Much of what they do in the classroom feels automatic, fluid, and natural. To them, their mastery is simply *teaching*.

How did they get so good? How did they become master teachers, and how can you become one yourself? The answer is that master teachers have learned how to rigorously apply a few simple principles of great teaching to their practice. They have, in short, developed a master teacher mindset.

The seven principles of mastery teaching are

1. Start where your students are.
2. Know where your students are going.
3. Expect to get your students to their goal.
4. Support your students along the way.
5. Use feedback to help you and your students get better.
6. Focus on quality rather than quantity.
7. Never work harder than your students.

As you can see, none of these principles is particularly earth shattering. They are things we all know intuitively that we should be doing in the classroom. But the master teacher mindset develops as a result of systematically and rigorously applying these principles to teaching until they become our spontaneous response to our students. The more you practice these principles, the more you too can begin to think like a master teacher, and the closer you will come to having a master teacher mindset.

How can you start to practice these principles in your own classroom? How can you do so in a way that is true to your own style and suits the learning needs of your particular students? How, in other words, can you systematically apply mastery principles to address the everyday challenges you face as a teacher? This series will show you what to do.

If you discovered this series through its companion book, *Never Work Harder Than Your Students and Other Principles of Great Teaching* (Jackson, 2009), you'll find some familiar concepts covered here. While *Never Work Harder Than Your Students* introduced the principles of mastery teaching, the how-to guides in the Mastering the Principles of Great Teaching series will take you step-by-step through the process of integrating those principles into your classroom practice and show you how to apply the principles to resolve specific teaching challenges you face.

Each of the how-to guides in this series focuses on one of the seven mastery principles. You'll examine the principle, assess your current practice of the principle, and learn new ways to incorporate it in your teaching. And because the series is designed to show the mastery principles in relation to specific teaching challenges, working your way through each guide will help you to resolve many of your immediate, day-to-day classroom challenges even as you build your overall mastery mindset.

Mastery teaching is not about fitting into a specific mold, and these guides are designed to help you grow no matter where you are in your practice. If you have read *Never Work Harder Than Your Students*, you may recall that it includes a diagnostic tool to help teachers assess their skill-level in each principle and locate themselves along a mastery teaching continuum ranging from novice to apprentice to practitioner to master teacher. Each of the how-to guides in this series also begins with a diagnostic tool to help you identify where you fall on the continuum so that you can focus specifically on the strategies best suited to your current practice. This format ensures that you will be able to work through all the guides at your own pace and level, cycle back through, and, with each rereading, deepen your understanding and further the development of your master teacher mindset.

The guides in the Mastering the Principles of Great Teaching series follow a standard format. After an introduction to the focus mastery principle and the diagnostic, you will work through a series of steps that prompt you to apply the principle rigorously and systematically to your classroom practice. Along the way, you will learn new strategies, develop new skills, and take time to reflect on your growth. The tools in each guide help you take a close look at your own teaching, examine your assumptions about teaching and how students learn, and refine your instruction so that your students can learn more effectively.

Becoming a master teacher has little to do with how many years you put in or how closely you resemble a particular Hollywood ideal. It isn't some special gift doled out at birth to only a chosen few. Any teacher can become a master teacher with the right kind of practice—the kind of practice this series of how-to guides offers. In working through them, you too can develop a master teacher mindset and be the master teacher your students deserve.

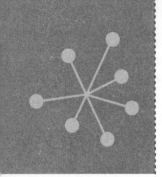

How to Use This Guide

There is plenty of advice out there on how to support struggling students. Unfortunately, much of this advice treats support like an add-on strategy and requires you to wait until after a student is in the cycle of failure before you intervene. Typical strategies and solutions focus on getting students back on track, but they rarely tell you how to keep students from struggling in the first place. This how-to guide takes a more comprehensive approach and will help you shift your stance from a *learning adversary* trying to "wring" the work out of a disengaged student to a *learning advocate* who works quickly and effectively to build students' capacity to successfully manage their own learning.

Focusing on the mastery principle "Support Your Students Along the Way," this guide outlines the key elements of a proactive support plan, shows you step-by-step how to build a support plan of your own, and provides tips and strategies to help you apply your support plan to your students and within the context of your classroom. Regardless of the grade level or discipline you teach, the concepts and strategies in this guide will help you support students as they learn and redirect students who show signs that they may be headed for failure.

How This Guide Is Structured

How to Support Struggling Students begins with an **Introduction** to the mastery principle and a **Self-Assessment**—a diagnostic tool to help you identify where your current application of the principle falls on the continuum of mastery teaching. Then, it's on to the guide's four chapters, each corresponding to a stage in the development of a proactive support plan:

- **Chapter 1: Supporting Students Before Instruction** shows you how to accelerate the students in your class by activating and creating background knowledge, preparing students with advance organizers, and helping them prelearn key vocabulary.

- **Chapter 2: Supporting Students During Instruction** explores productive and destructive struggle as part of the learning process. You will learn how to establish "red flags" to identify when students' struggle has become destructive and how to link these red flags to targeted interventions that quickly get struggling students back on course.

- **Chapter 3: Supporting Students After Instruction** offers ideas for meaningful remediation for the few students who do not achieve mastery even with acceleration and intervention.

- **Chapter 4: Putting It All Together** prompts you to draw connections between the reading and guided practice you have completed and your support plans for your own students and classroom.

Throughout the guide, **Your Turn** sections provide suggestions for how you can begin to take action in your own classroom. We have divided these suggestions into four levels, keyed to readers' current application of the principle:

- *Aquire.* The suggestions here will help teachers working at the novice level develop a better understanding of the principle and of their own teaching practice as it relates to the principle.

- *Apply.* The suggestions here focus on showing teachers working at the apprentice level how to use the guide's strategies in their teaching practice.

- *Assimilate.* The suggestions here present teachers working at the practitioner level with additional ideas about how to incorporate the principle and strategies into their existing practice.

- *Adapt.* The suggestions here will help teachers working at the master teacher level take a fresh look at their own practice and use some of the guide's strategies in a way that's right for them and their students.

Think of this guide like a spiral staircase in which you return to the same concepts more than once, each time pushing yourself to an incrementally higher level as you proceed toward mastery. The breaks between each level are natural "rest stops"—places where you will know you've made substantial progress and can pause so that you won't feel overwhelmed or stuck before moving forward. Rest assured, even if you don't move beyond the *Acquire* suggestions your first time through the guide, you will still have made progress. Stop there and try those skills out in your classroom. Then, as your ability and confidence grow, you can return to this guide with your next unit or next semester in mind. Each time you will continue enhancing your practice by ramping up to the apprentice level and beyond as you build your master teacher mindset and refine your practice.

Tools

Throughout this guide, you'll also find other tools to help you reach your goals, including

 Checklists outlining what each chapter will help you accomplish.

 Time-Saving Tips to steer you toward information that will allow you to complete the work in each chapter more quickly.

 Checkpoint Summaries that quickly summarize key content. You can use these to assess your own understanding of specific concepts and as a handy reminder.

 Take It Step by Step boxes that summarize the key steps in a process.

 Learn More Online sections that point you to other strategies and additional resources available on the web.

Think About sections that raise reflection questions prompting you to consider what you've read and make connections to your own classroom and teaching practice.

 Yes, But . . . sections addressing common objections and reservations teachers sometimes express in relation to these strategies. These sections will help you resolve some practical challenges and overcome hesitation you might be feeling.

You will also find a variety of worksheets, planning templates, and strategy sheets that will help you capture your learning and build a comprehensive plan. The **Appendixes** at the end of the guide offer a set of sample comprehensive proactive support plans for elementary, middle, and high school students, as well as a sample parent support contract illustrating an effective way to communicate your plan to both parents and students.

Your Approach

If you are working through this how-to guide individually, we recommend you first take time to understand the book's general framework. Preview the material and make a commitment to spend a certain amount of time each week working through the various chapters. You can read all the way through before deciding where to begin, or you can jump right in and start trying some of the strategies outlined. Either way, be sure to reflect periodically on how applying these strategies affects your practice and your students. Then adjust your practice accordingly.

If you are working through this guide with other teachers in a small-group setting, begin with an overview of the various chapters and discuss which of the practices within might give each group member the most trouble and which of the practices members are more comfortable or experienced with. Use this information to designate a group facilitator for each chapter in order to keep everyone focused and on track. Then make some commitments as a group about how you will work through the chapters individually and meet regularly to discuss your progress, share your triumphs, and brainstorm ways around your challenges. You can use the "Think About" sections as a starting point for group discussion and then share individual strategies that you have implemented in the classroom.

If you are an administrator or teacher leader, this guide will give you a wonderful snapshot of the kinds of effective support practices that should be happening in every classroom. And it will provide you with useful tools you can offer to teachers as you conference with them and support their professional development.

Share Your Progress

As always, we want to hear from you! Contact us at info@mindstepsinc.com to ask questions, share your experiences, and pass along success stories of how you've made a difference in supporting struggling students. Administrators and district-level leaders are welcome to contact us to learn more about the supports Mindsteps Inc. offers for teachers and schools; give us a call at 1-888-565-8881 or send us an e-mail. We would love to help.

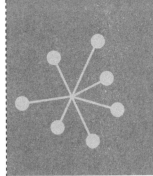

Self-Assessment: Supporting Your Students

Answer each of the follow questions as honestly as you can; don't think about what you would like to do but about what you currently do in your own practice. There are no right or wrong answers.

1. If asked to describe my practice in general terms, I would say
   a. I am still learning my discipline and try to stay at least one step ahead of my students.
   b. I understand my discipline well enough to teach it, although there are times when I get stumped as to how to explain something to a student.
   c. For the most part I understand my discipline and have more than one way of explaining the major concepts to students.
   d. I understand my discipline and take time to explain not only the concepts and skills to my students but also the ways of knowing in my particular subject.

2. Before the unit begins, I most often support students by
   a. Giving them a study guide that outlines how the unit will proceed.
   b. Telling them that they can come in for extra help if they need to.
   c. Previewing key vocabulary, strategies, and background knowledge.
   d. Developing tiered assignments based on students' abilities and interests.

3. When a student seems to misunderstand a concept, I typically
   a. Press ahead and hope that the student will understand later.
   b. Try to understand why the student is getting confused and then work to clear up his confusion during the lesson.
   c. Try to get to the student after school or during lunch to clear up his confusion.
   d. Give the student an alternate reading or supplementary materials to help clear up his confusion.

4. I decide what is acceptable mastery based on
   a. The students' grades. A passing grade means they have mastered the material.
   b. A baseline measure provided in the curriculum standard.
   c. The students' test scores. A passing grade on the summative assessment means they have mastered the material.
   d. The students' grades. Earning an *A* or a *B* in the class means they have mastered the material.

5. I decide how to help a struggling student
   a. Before that student begins to struggle.
   b. At the first sign the student is struggling (usually a failed quiz or test).
   c. Once the student has shown that she is failing (usually at the interim-report stage).
   d. Once the student has failed the marking period.

6. When planning my lessons, I can predict where students are most likely to become confused based on
   a. What material seems to have the most explanation in the curriculum guide.
   b. What material was confusing to my students in the past.
   c. What I know about my subject, and where students are in their conceptual development.
   d. What I know about my subject and the most common misconceptions about the material.

From *Never Work Harder Than Your Students and Other Principles of Great Teaching* by R. R. Jackson, 2009. Alexandria, VA: ASCD. Copyright 2009 by Robyn R. Jackson. Adapted with permission.

7. If a student fails a test, I typically
 a. Figure out why the student failed and offer remediation.
 b. Record the grade.
 c. Offer extra-credit opportunities to help offset the low grade.
 d. Institute some corrective action and give the student the opportunity to retake the test.

8. I know that a student is struggling in my class when
 a. The student fails a quiz, test, or some other assessment.
 b. The student asks for help.
 c. The student triggers a predetermined red flag.
 d. The student is earning a failing grade at mid-term.

Scoring

For each question, circle the number in the column that represents your answer. For instance, if you answered B for question 1, you would circle the 2. When you have finished, calculate the totals for each column and then determine your grand total by adding up the four column totals.

Question	A	B	C	D	
1	1	2	3	4	
2	2	1	4	3	
3	1	2	3	4	
4	1	4	3	2	
5	4	3	2	1	
6	1	2	4	3	
7	3	1	2	4	
8	3	1	4	2	Grand Total
Total					

Going Forward

Use your grand total to determine your current level of principle application, and locate the most appropriate suggestions for taking action in your own classroom.

8–11 points: Novice

If you scored in the novice range, focus on the **Acquire** suggestions. If the content and practices there are familiar, feel free to jump to the next level and look at the suggestions under the *Apply, Assimilate*, and *Adapt* headings. As you build your confidence with the Acquire actions, return to this book and work through it again at a different level.

12–19 points: Apprentice

If you scored in the apprentice range, focus on the **Apply** suggestions. Try out some of the strategies with a small unit of study and pay attention to how they work for your students. As you become more comfortable applying these skills to your practice, move to the *Assimilate* suggestions for those strategies that work best for you and your students. If you have been using some of the *Apply* practices, you may want to start at the *Assimilate* or *Adapt* levels and refine what you are already doing.

20–27 points: Practitioner

If you scored in the practitioner range, focus on the **Assimilate** suggestions. Look for ways to begin integrating more of this guide's recommended strategies into your overall practice so that this support of students becomes more automatic and comprehensive. If a particular practice is new to you, start at the *Acquire* or *Apply* suggestions and work your way up to those under *Assimilate*. If a practice is embedded into your teaching habits already, try some suggestions associated with the *Adapt* heading.

28–32 points: Master Teacher

If you scored in the master teacher range, focus on the **Adapt** suggestions. Many of the support measures in this book are already part of your regular classroom philosophy and practice. Start with the *Adapt* suggestions and customize them to your students and your classroom context. If you come across a strategy that is new to you, take time to work through the *Acquire, Adapt*, and *Assimilate* steps so that it too can become a seamless part of your overall practice.

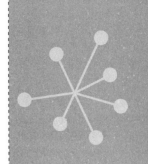

Introduction:
Understanding the Mastery Principle

If we want our students to succeed, we cannot afford to leave to chance what happens when they do not learn.

All teachers have had that moment in the classroom where we've just finished explaining what we thought was a simple concept and then see our students staring blankly back, completely lost. We all know the sinking feeling that comes with realizing that, in spite of our best efforts, our students still don't understand our lesson. And we have all experienced the frustration that comes when students continue to struggle and constantly lag behind. There is curriculum to cover and a test to give, and students just aren't keeping up.

Often we don't intervene until after students have shown us that they don't understand. Then we look for some sort of remediation so they can "relearn" what they failed to absorb the first time, or we slow down and work at a pace we think they can handle. For both teachers and students, it's a reactive cycle of catching on and catching up that can be as exhausting as it is disheartening.

But what if we could catch students the moment that they began to struggle and help them quickly get back on track? What if we could build-in support systems that would prevent more of them from struggling at all? What if there was something we could do to make student success a lot more likely?

The Curse of Knowledge

The problem is, once a person knows something, it is really difficult to understand what it is like *not* to know it. Often teachers' understanding of a concept or process makes it next to impossible for us to imagine what it is like for students who do not have that same understanding. Think back to learning to drive. The first time you backed out of the driveway, you had to coach yourself to check your mirrors, look over your shoulder, ease off the brake, and decide which way to turn the steering wheel in order to make the car go where you wanted it to. Now you can probably do the same task while talking to a passenger and drinking a cup of coffee.

As teachers, we face the "curse of knowledge" all the time in our classrooms. What seems easy and obvious to us can be inscrutable for our students. But we can learn how to use the curse of knowledge to our advantage. If we are aware of it, we can work to anticipate where our students may become confused and figure out how to deliver truly effective instruction.

Proactive Support

Proactive support guides students throughout the learning process, keeping them moving toward mastery and getting them quickly back on track when they struggle. Instead of merely giving students the opportunity to learn, proactive support puts structures in place to make mastery the inevitable result for most students most of the time. Much like the more formal structure of Response to Intervention (RTI), proactive support provides a series of progressive, systematic, just-in-time responses to students before, during, and after the lesson to ensure that students consistently get the help they need until they are successful. Figure 1 illustrates the process.

Providing students with support before the lesson prepares them for learning. If we set students up to learn, if we help them acquire the skills they will need to learn effectively the first time, far fewer of them will encounter difficulty. Even when students are well prepared, inevitably there will be points along the way where they may become confused; the trick is to anticipate where these difficulties may lie and then be ready with effective intervention. A few students, despite your best efforts and support, will still struggle. Setting up opportunities prior to the summative assessment for students to re-engage with the material and to learn the things they missed provides yet another chance to ensure that all of your students master the material.

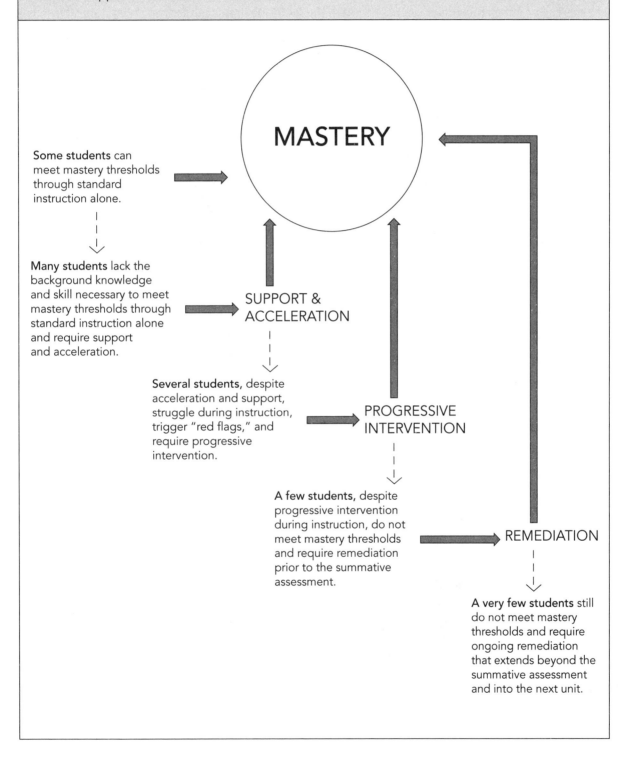

Figure 1. Master teachers develop a system of targeted, progressive responses designed to keep most students succeeding most of the time while providing targeted interventions for those students who appear to be headed for failure.

MASTERY

Some students can meet mastery thresholds through standard instruction alone.

Many students lack the background knowledge and skill necessary to meet mastery thresholds through standard instruction alone and require support and acceleration.

SUPPORT & ACCELERATION

Several students, despite acceleration and support, struggle during instruction, trigger "red flags," and require progressive intervention.

PROGRESSIVE INTERVENTION

A few students, despite progressive intervention during instruction, do not meet mastery thresholds and require remediation prior to the summative assessment.

REMEDIATION

A very few students still do not meet mastery thresholds and require ongoing remediation that extends beyond the summative assessment and into the next unit.

Giving students both preventive and targeted, just-in-time support also helps you. Teaching can be frustrating, particularly when some or all of the students in your class seem to lag behind, give up too easily, or resist the work habits that could make them much more successful. Although the methods in this guide won't eliminate all frustration from your professional life, they will build your capacity to deliver instruction in a way that encourages student progress.

Making time to reflect on your practice and incorporate the methods and strategies in this book can yield rich rewards in your classroom day to day. As students come to understand how the safety nets and interventions built into your instruction operate, they will be better able to stay on course or quickly redirect themselves when they begin to struggle. Having a clear and objective plan for intervention allows teachers to make academic support appear . . . supportive. All too often students add to their struggle by resisting help because it feels like punishment. As students' knowledge and confidence increase, the classroom becomes a much more productive and positive place to be.

✓ CHECKPOINT SUMMARY

Effective Support IS...	Effective Support Is NOT...
Ongoing Proactive Targeted Accelerative Learning focused Managed by a teacher as advocate	As needed Reactive Generalized Remedial Behavior focused Imposed by a teacher as adversary

THINK ABOUT . . .

Take a moment to reflect and write down a few notes. Who are your struggling students this year? How or why do they seem to struggle? What have you tried so far? Which support strategies seem to work best?

Supporting Students
Before Instruction

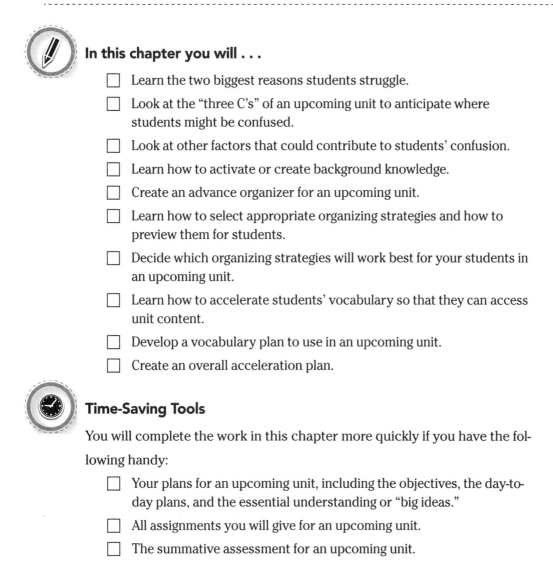

In this chapter you will . . .

- ☐ Learn the two biggest reasons students struggle.
- ☐ Look at the "three C's" of an upcoming unit to anticipate where students might be confused.
- ☐ Look at other factors that could contribute to students' confusion.
- ☐ Learn how to activate or create background knowledge.
- ☐ Create an advance organizer for an upcoming unit.
- ☐ Learn how to select appropriate organizing strategies and how to preview them for students.
- ☐ Decide which organizing strategies will work best for your students in an upcoming unit.
- ☐ Learn how to accelerate students' vocabulary so that they can access unit content.
- ☐ Develop a vocabulary plan to use in an upcoming unit.
- ☐ Create an overall acceleration plan.

Time-Saving Tools

You will complete the work in this chapter more quickly if you have the following handy:

- ☐ Your plans for an upcoming unit, including the objectives, the day-to-day plans, and the essential understanding or "big ideas."
- ☐ All assignments you will give for an upcoming unit.
- ☐ The summative assessment for an upcoming unit.
- ☐ Any curriculum guides for the unit provided by your school or district.

Now that you understand the principle, how will you help students reach mastery? The first step is to figure out how you will support students before the lesson or unit even begins.

Why do students struggle in school? Generally, it is because they lack either the background knowledge or the "soft skills" they need to acquire and retain new information.

Students who struggle because of a lack of background knowledge don't have the vocabulary or the experiences they need to make sense of new information. Without an understanding of the vocabulary and without the experiences that provide context, they have nothing on which to "hook" the new knowledge. This kind of prior knowledge is vital for reading comprehension and critical thinking, and without it, students are at a serious disadvantage.

"Soft skills" are the skills that support learning, such as note taking, study skills, and organization. Students who lack these tools are able to learn, but the process of learning required by many classrooms mystifies them. They do not know how to take notes in a way that facilitates review, they do not know how to study from their notes, they don't know how to ask for help when they struggle, and they may not even know how to monitor themselves in order to recognize that they are not making progress.

Many students would struggle much less in school if, before we presented new material for them to learn, we took the time to help them acquire background knowledge and skills that will help them learn. Acceleration strategies that preview content and the skills ensure a proper foundation for new learning. Investing time in teaching students *how* to learn is never wasted; in doing so, you deepen their understanding of the upcoming content and better equip them for future success.

Why We Shouldn't Wait to Intervene

Instead of addressing the root causes of student failure—lack of prior knowledge and lack of soft skills—most supports we provide for students attempt to address specific, identified deficits. We work to help students complete particular assignments, for example, or try to reteach everything the student did not get the first time. But if we wait for kids to fail before we intervene, we are setting them up for even more failure. The research shows that the longer students stay in traditional remedial programs, the further they fall below grade level (Thompson, Thompson, & Thompson, 2005). When you think about it, remediation is really taking students backward rather than forward. And the more that they are backward-focused, trying to catch up and keep up at the same time, the more frustrated they become and the more hopeless they feel.

Waiting for students to fail before providing them with the support they need also creates another problem. If students are having difficulty understanding a concept and we wait until the unit is over to go over that concept again and provide them with support, they have to restart their study of that concept at the same time we are asking them to master the concepts in a new unit. With instruction that is so disjointed, they are likely to have an even harder time learning.

One of the biggest problems associated with not intervening until after students have failed is that the experience of academic failure significantly lowers students' self-esteem and sense of efficacy. They lose confidence in their ability to learn. They begin to believe that they can't do any better and that they will always be behind. They often just give up. The research tells us that self-esteem and self-efficacy account for about 50 percent of students' achievement (Thompson et al., 2005). By allowing students to fail before we begin to intervene, we are actually limiting their chances of success. Instead of asking how we can help our students catch up, we should be asking how we can make learning more likely the first time around.

Anticipating Confusion

The answer is to look forward, not backward. It is much better to anticipate areas of difficulty and begin thinking through how we will keep more of our students on track.

Picture yourself as the eye-in-the-sky helicopter or traffic camera operator. All of your students are zooming along the highway toward the big summative test or project. They see only what's in front of them, but from your vantage point you can tell when one or more of them has veered in the wrong direction, stalled out, or gotten turned around. Anticipating confusion will lay the foundation for your preplanning of supports and give you opportunities to clear up that confusion before the lesson. It will better prepare you to intervene the moment students begin to struggle.

There are many ways to determine which students will struggle and what they will struggle with. One way is to look at the "three C's" of learning: concept, content, and context.

Concept is a term used to refer to a "big idea" or an "enduring understanding." Concepts are those underlying and essential ideas that unify and link the facts, details, principles, formulas, and procedures in your curriculum. Thinking through a concept helps you anticipate where students might be confused. What are the common misunderstandings that exist for this concept? What are the common errors students make when trying to master this concept? Rather than waiting for students to develop these misunderstandings or make these errors, why not design your instruction to prevent them altogether?

Content has to do with all the information and processes you will use to help students acquire the concepts addressed in your unit. Does the story you have selected have vocabulary that may be unfamiliar to some students? Do the math problems you have selected require that students have their multiplication table memorized? Does the region you have selected for study require students to have some familiarity with its history or culture? Does the piece you want students to play require that they also understand a particular key signature? Examine your content and look for the background knowledge your students will need in order to access it successfully. Doing so will not only help you anticipate potential areas of confusion but also tell you what type of acceleration strategies you should use to prepare students to engage with the selected content.

Context addresses the means through which students access learning. Once you decide what concepts students will learn and what content will facilitate that learning, you need to think about the context in which you will ask students to learn. Will you require them to read a chapter in the textbook? Participate in a discovery lab? Work in cooperative groups? Take notes during a film?

Thinking through the context ahead of time allows you to identify the skills that students will need. Focus on what students have to be able to do in order to succeed in that particular learning context. When you identify the skills a particular context implies, you can anticipate where students are likely to require support and what kind of support to plan for.

Much of anticipating confusion is a matter of considering the interplay of the three C's. Select an upcoming lesson or unit you will teach within the next six weeks, and use the guiding questions in the **Anticipating Confusion Worksheet** on the next page to think through the concept, content and processes, and context. For now, just jot down your ideas. These are the starting points you will develop further as you work through the rest of the worksheets in this guide.

In addition to thinking about the unit's three C's, you should also think about your students. If you have worked with this group of students for some time, or if you have taught this same course more than once, you probably have an idea of where students are likely to struggle. Take a look at the list below and consider some of the other ways that you could anticipate confusion. As you read, you might want to put a checkmark beside methods you currently use, an arrow beside those you would like to start using, and a question mark beside those you feel uncertain about.

- *Consider students with identified needs.* Students with IEPs or 504 plans usually come into our classrooms with documented needs and accommodations. It's likely that when your curriculum overlaps with a student's documented special needs, that student will need support and accommodation.

- *Consider special populations.* If students with limited English proficiency are part of your classroom, you can anticipate that they will need targeted support when it comes to vocabulary-intensive material, writing, academic language, and content that builds on prior knowledge of U.S. history or culture.

- *Consider performance prior to the course.* If some students in your class have not demonstrated proficiency in reading, in math, or on other standardized tests in the past, it is likely they will require support in these areas as they relate to your course.

Anticipating Confusion Worksheet

	Your Unit	Your Analysis
Concept	In this unit, what are the key concepts your students need to understand in order to reach mastery?	What are the common misunderstandings of this concept?
Content/Process	What content or processes will help students understand these concepts?	What prior knowledge and vocabulary will students need to access this content?
Context	In which contexts will you ask students to learn the key concepts?	What skills will students need in order to be successful in these contexts? What kind of thinking and organizational strategies does each context demand?

- ***Consider performance during the course.*** If you have already worked with this group of students for a few weeks or even a couple of marking periods, think about the students who have struggled to meet standards in your course up to this point. Data from past grades, observation, and even conversation with students can be a strong indicator of which students will need support.

A student who had difficulty breaking down complex tasks, managing time, or organizing writing last marking period will probably need support in the same areas this marking period. Try to stick to the facts and avoid assigning blame or negative attributes. You might be tempted to think, *Alyssa got a* D *last quarter because she didn't turn in her essays; she's lazy, so I should work on her laziness.* Better, though, to focus on factors that are more likely to be within your control: *Alyssa got a* D *because she didn't turn in her essays. When we get to the essay this quarter, I will provide supports to Alyssa to help ensure she turns in her essay.*

- ***Consider historically difficult concepts or assignments.*** Whether you're teaching this course for the second, third, or thirteenth time, reflect on the places that former students got lost or confused and build in supports to minimize confusion and frustration for current students. As you teach, think about keeping a running list of material or assignments that confuse students and which elements of your instruction, directions, class format, or presentation could have gone more smoothly. Keep that document with your materials for the unit so that when you get to the same point next year, you can avoid repeating the things that didn't work.

- ***Consider student reflection and goals.*** As students move through the grades and become more mature, they are often able to identify and anticipate areas of confusion or frustration themselves. Provide students with structures that will help them reflect on their performance, alert you to content or processes that typically frustrate or confuse them, and set learning goals that address these areas.

- ***Consider data from pre-assessments.*** As you become more comfortable with defining mastery and quickly responding to students who are slipping below the mastery threshold, you will probably want to begin using diagnostic pre-assessments at the beginning of each new unit. Pre-assessments should cover a range of specific content and skills that are central to a new unit. While these pre-assessments are not to be included in a student's grade, they can yield valuable data about what each student already knows and where the gaps in knowledge and skills lie. Pre-assessment data signal a teacher early on as to which students may need support or intervention and which may be ready for more challenging extension activities.

- ***Consider data from ongoing assessments.*** Both formal and informal assessment data you collect during the instructional process will let you know which students are mastering material, which students are struggling, and where the areas of confusion lie.

THINK ABOUT . . .

Think ahead to your next lesson sequence or unit. Make note of a few concepts or assignments you anticipate will confuse students. Write down the names of specific students you think will be confused or off-track and why.

YOUR TURN

Acquire: If you are teaching particular concepts for the first time, it is tough to anticipate where students might be confused. Start by thinking about the common misconceptions that exist about each of these concepts. What are some of the mistakes everyone tends to make when learning about it? Then, as you teach, make note of areas where students seem to be confused or have difficulty. Save these notes for when you teach the topic again so that you can be more deliberate about anticipating confusion.

Apply: Think back to when you taught these concepts last and try to remember where students got confused or encountered difficulty. What will you do differently this time around to prevent or minimize their confusion?

Assimilate: Think about what you do now to keep students from being confused during particular lessons. Refer to the list of suggestions on page 26, and select one or two other ways you could help prevent or minimize confusion.

Adapt: Think about the students in your class who chronically struggle. What areas in an upcoming lesson might be particularly difficult for them? What additional supports could you provide to help these students keep up with the rest of the class? How might you work with a coteacher or use the assistance of other students to provide these supports?

Acceleration

If your students are struggling because they lack prior knowledge, have limited vocabulary and experiences, demonstrate acute gaps in their learning, or have not developed the soft skills they need to learn effectively, it is important to use acceleration to equip them with these tools. Acceleration rounds out students' background knowledge and helps them develop more effective strategies for acquiring and retaining information.

Acceleration is not the same as preteaching. When we preteach a lesson, we typically use many of the same strategies and assignments that we go on to use in the actual lesson. While preteaching is focused on giving students multiple exposures to the content, acceleration is really more about foundation work. It's a way to help students develop the *prerequisite* knowledge and skills they need to be successful with the lesson material. Acceleration might include introducing important vocabulary, providing advance organizers, using activating strategies or student learning maps, and filling in important background knowledge. It directly addresses the major causes for students' difficulty in school—lack of background knowledge and soft skills—by helping students acquire and develop the knowledge and skills they are missing.

There are three key components to acceleration: *activating or creating backgound knowledge*, *providing and previewing organizing strategies*, and *teaching vocabulary.*

Activating or Creating Background Knowledge

Learning is a lot like hook-and-loop tape. In order for it to stick, students need hooks in their brains on which they can loop new information. Students who lack the proper background knowledge for the learning they're tasked with do not have the hooks that will grab on to the new information and make it stick.

Activating activities are designed to tease out what students already know or think they know about a topic. It's a powerful support strategy because it gives students a reference point: a place to begin and a frame for comparison. Instead of learning everything from scratch, they can leverage what they know already and make deeper connections between that knowledge and upcoming unit content.

Activating prior knowledge can also be very motivating. Sometimes when students encounter a new unit, they are intimidated by how much they will have to learn. By reminding them of what they know already, you can make the learning task before them seem much more doable. When you activate prior knowledge, you get students warmed up, focused, and ready to learn.

Finally, activating strategies can reveal—and allow you to address—key gaps in students' understanding or any misconceptions about a topic that may get in the way of new learning.

LEARN MORE Online

Strategies for Activating Prior Knowledge

- KWL Outlines
- Anticipation Guides
- Prereading Plans
- Directed Reading Activities
- Word Splashes
- Carousel Brainstorming
- Statement Strategy
- Paired Verbal Fluency
- Semantic Mapping

Strategies for Creating Background Knowledge

- Showing a topic-related movie or movie clip
- Assigning a children's book on the topic to provide a rudimentary overview
- Sending students to a website focused on key information they will need to understand.
- Process simulations
- Using analogies to connect what students are about to learn with something that they know already
- Minilessons covering specific necessary concepts or skills

You can download details on these strategies at www.mindstepsinc.com/support.

To activate prior knowledge, use strategies that help students link what they know already with what they are about to learn. If students are preparing to learn the causes of World War II, for example, help them recall what they learned about the causes of World War I. If they are beginning to multiply fractions, refresh their thinking on adding and subtracting fractions so they can note similarities and differences of the new process. If they are learning to write using action verbs and colorful modifiers, choose a passage from a text they've already read, and review and analyze it, calling students' attention to these particular constructions.

While activating prior knowledge is a great strategy to help students begin to make connections between what they know already and what they are about to learn, the reason many students struggle with new learning is because they are *missing* that critical background knowledge. They don't have the right hooks. These students might not have had the opportunity to learn the material, or they may have failed to learn it because of problems related to attention or motivation, to vocabulary deficits, or to memory problems. In such cases, you have to think critically about the concepts the lesson will address and quickly create the background knowledge they will need to engage with lesson content. For instance, before beginning a unit on a specific country's government or culture, you could have students watch a clip from a movie set in that country to get them thinking about what life is like there. You could have students read a children's book that quickly explains a scientific or mathematics concept that will be critical to their understanding of an upcoming lesson. You could show students an online simulation as a way of helping them see a process before you introduce it to them in class. You could provide an article or textbook passage designed for younger children that gives a simple overview. You could use metaphors or analogies that help students see how what they are about to learn is similar to something that they already know.

Be careful here. You want to help students develop critical background knowledge, but you can't reteach everything students should have learned prior to coming to your class. There just isn't time for that. Instead, think about what knowledge and skills students absolutely must have in order to be successful with the coming unit. What do they need to know in order to carry out the critical thinking the unit activities require? What background knowledge will inform their understanding of the concepts they are about to learn?

Also keep in mind that students do not need deep background knowledge in order to engage in the critical thinking tasks you will require. Even a shallow exposure to information will help them create the learning hooks on which to hang upcoming information.

Now it's time to try your hand at identifying critical background knowledge and possible activating strategies for a unit you teach. Take a look at the sample activation plan on the next page, and then complete the **Activation Plan Worksheet** on page 29. Start by returning to the Anticipating Confusion Worksheet you completed on page 22 and pulling in one of the key concepts you identified there. Next look at what you wrote in the "Your Analysis" column. What background knowledge will students need in order to access the content? How will you help students recall that prior learning? What will you do if students demonstrate that they cannot recall or have never been exposed to critical background knowledge? See the list of strategies on page 26 for ideas.

Sample Activation Plan

Key Concept

Geometric figures are similar when corresponding angles are congruent and when the lengths of corresponding sides are proportional.

Background Knowledge

Ratios	Measurement	Parts of a Whole
• Defining ratios • Solving for x in ratios	• Angles • Length	• Fractions • Equivalent Fractions

Activating Strategy

Statement strategy on the concept of ratios with true and false statements about ratios to help uncover any misconceptions students have about ratios Warm-up activity in which students solve for x as practice	Group activity in which students measure the different angles on a worksheet, to be followed by a class discussion of angles Students who need more background knowledge will read The Greedy Triangle by Marilyn Burns to learn about key geometry concepts	Word splash showing how fractions, ratios, and measurement relate to the concept of proportions

Activation Plan Worksheet

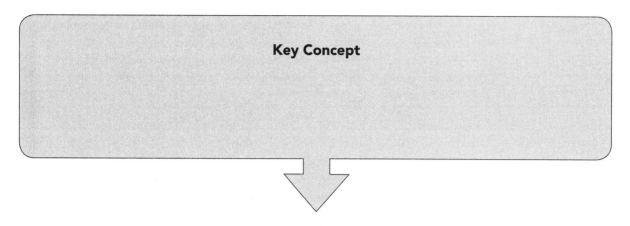

THINK ABOUT . . .

Consider a lesson you have taught in which some students didn't have the background knowledge you assumed they would have. How did that gap affect the lesson? What "on the spot" corrections did you have to make? Now think about an upcoming lesson in which students may have insufficient background knowledge. How can you plan beforehand to address the gap?

YOUR TURN

Acquire: Consider the introductory lesson for an upcoming unit or lesson sequence. Identify the concepts, content/processes, and context that may confuse students or about which they may have limited background knowledge. Then identify one strategy you will use to help activate students' prior knowledge before the lesson. Start collecting other activating strategies you can use with students.

Apply: Look ahead to all the lessons in an upcoming mini-unit or lesson sequence. Determine what strategy you will use to activate students' background knowledge. Then, identify the content and processes about which students have limited background knowledge. Select one strategy you will use to help create background knowledge for students. Begin using additional activating strategies with students in future lessons.

Assimilate: Look ahead to all the lessons in an upcoming unit. Using formative assessment strategies and recalling your own experience with students, identify the content and processes about which students have limited background knowledge. Next, think about the strategies you typically use to activate or create background knowledge for students. Identify parts of the lessons where it would be beneficial to include more activities strategies and select one or more of the strategies on page 26 to use with students in the upcoming unit.

YOUR TURN, cont.

Adapt: In addition to thinking about how you will activate prior knowledge in your current unit, look ahead to the units you plan for the semester or the year. What knowledge will you need to help students build now so that they will be able to access future units?

Providing and Previewing Organizing Strategies

The research tells us that "successful learning involves the use of numerous strategies for organizing, storing, and internalizing knowledge" (Thompson et al., 2005, p. 13). Sharing organizing strategies is a way to help ensure that students know *how* to learn before you *ask* them to learn. For this reason, it is good policy to provide students with the organizing strategies they will need for an upcoming unit before the unit begins.

For example, if you know that students will need to take notes in your class, you might demonstrate or explain a note-taking strategy in advance so that when it is time for them to take notes, they will know exactly what kind of information they should focus on capturing. Or if reading a chapter in the textbook or a short story is part of your lesson plan, you might review with students the various strategies that will help them identify the important information and pick up on the key points.

Although there are other organizing strategies you might use and share with students, the most powerful one is the use of graphic organizers. What makes graphic organizers so valuable is their plasticity: they can mirror the thinking processes we want our students to adopt and clarify the relationships we want them to notice and understand.

Suppose you want your students to use the notes they take in order to marshal evidence for an upcoming persuasive essay. Graphic organizers can show students how to organize their evidence to support their thesis. Perhaps you want your students to notice patterns among several examples. Graphic organizers can prompt students to identify the commonalities among these examples and lead students to extrapolate patterns. Or maybe you simply want students to be able to capture information they encounter in text, via a lecture, or online in a format that will make the information easier to access and remember. Graphic organizers for note taking provide helpful structures for doing just that.

Graphic organizers can also support reading comprehension and foster critical reading skill. For instance, most textbook chapters are organized by either cause/effect, compare/contrast, or sequence—be it procedural or historical. Many students miss key points because they are not aware of these structures. Thus, they might take notes sequentially when the chapter is actually comparing two things, or they might infer cause and effect when there is none. Simply giving students a note-taking graphic organizer that makes the underlying organizational structure of the chapter explicit can help them understand the content better.

TAKE IT STEP BY STEP

How to Preview Organizing Strategies

1. Examine your content and select an organizing strategy consistent with the thinking skills involved.
2. One week prior to the unit's beginning, introduce students to the organizing strategy.
3. Over the next week, conduct minilessons or warm-up activities to help students practice the organizing strategies.
4. Point out to students how using the strategy can help them organize their thinking.

Graphic organizers can be used to help students sort out their thoughts before a writing assignment, summarize what they are learning, and link what they have learned to what they are about to learn. Regardless of the organizing strategy you use, previewing organizing strategies involves several short steps. First, take a look at the context you have in mind for an upcoming unit and decide what organizational strategies would help students be successful in that context. What thinking skills will be required? How will students need to organize what they are learning in order to think in the way that the lesson demands? These are the organizing skills you will need to teach students prior to the lesson.

About a week before the unit begins, introduce students to the organizing or thinking strategy. Show students how it works and what kind of thinking it supports. Discuss with students why they would use that particular strategy and the pros and cons for using it.

Next, during several minilessons and warm-up activities throughout the week, have students practice the strategy using material that is easy for them to understand. Talk with students about how the organizing strategy is a tool they can use to learn more effectively. The clearer their understanding of this point, the more likely they will be to actually use the strategy once the lesson gets underway.

We want to stress that the key to preparing students to use effective strategies as they learn is to give them plenty of practice and feedback on how to use the strategy *before* they need to use it. This approach lets them develop and refine the skills they need to facilitate their learning without also having to manage the learning task itself.

For example, suppose you wanted to teach students the difference between a solar and a lunar eclipse. That is your concept. Your context is that you are going to ask students to read a textbook chapter about both types of eclipses in preparation for a class discussion. During the discussion, you expect your students to be able to give at least three similarities and three differences between the two types of eclipses and to do so both orally and in writing. As you analyze the context, you determine that students will need to know how to take notes from the text and use those notes in a class discussion in order to participate in the class discussion effectively. A Venn diagram, you decide, is the best graphic organizer for the job; it will help students organize their notes into similarities and differences and, thus, facilitate their ability to access this information during the class discussion.

About a week before the reading assignment, take a few minutes at the end of class to show students how to use a Venn diagram. The next day, during a minilesson, ask students as a class to complete a Venn diagram covering the similarities and differences of two things that interest them: their two favorite television shows, perhaps, or soccer and football. A few days later (the day before the reading assignment), as a warm-up activity, ask students to read a short passage in which two items are compared, take notes in pairs, and then compare notes with another pair. Next, as a class, discuss how they completed the Venn diagram and how they selected which items to compare. Refer to the clues available in the text passage—words like "versus" or "similarly," for example, or phrases like "as opposed to." Then, on the day of the chapter reading assignment, remind students of how they used the Venn diagram and tell them to use the tool as they read the textbook chapter for homework.

Now it's time for you to try this approach and plan how you will preview an organizing strategy with students for an upcoming lesson or unit. Complete the **Pre-viewing Organizing Strategies Worksheet** on the next page, using the information you recorded in the Anticipating Confusion Worksheet on page 22 as a starting point. Remember that you will need to accomplish everything within the week prior to the lesson in which students will need to use the organizing strategy.

THINK ABOUT . . .

How have you organized your unit's content? How might you show that underlying organization to your students? Take a look at some of the graphic organizers at www. mindstepsinc.com/support. What are some strategies that students can use to organize the information they are learning? How can you teach students these strategies ahead of time?

YOUR TURN

Acquire: Start collecting graphic organizers you can use with your students. Visit www.mindstepsinc.com/support for a list and instructions.

Assimilate: Start building organizing strategies into your lessons. Devote at least one warm-up activity or "do now" a week to practicing an organizing strategy with students.

Apply: Think about what organizing strategies you are already using with your students. Look for other areas where an organizing strategy will promote the kinds of deep thinking you want your students to engage in during a lesson, and teach these additional strategies to students.

Adapt: Look across multiple units or subject areas in which you teach. Identify patterns in organizational strategies, and work to provide students with experience using various organizers.

Previewing Organizing Strategies Worksheet

Key Concept:	
1. In **which context** will students learn the content of the lesson or unit?	
2. What kind of **thinking** does the context demand? Will students need to take notes? How will they be asked to use their notes? Will students need to read? For what purpose?	
3. How will you **introduce the strategy** to students?	
4. What are the **pros and cons** for using this strategy?	
5. **How does this strategy help students be more successful** with the lesson or unit?	
6. How will students **practice** the strategy?	
7. How will students ultimately **use** the strategy?	

Teaching Vocabulary

Vocabulary is critical to learning because it is what allows us to take an experience, store it in memory, and recount it later. Without a strong vocabulary, students have trouble thinking abstractly and retaining information. If your students are reading but not comprehending the textbook, if their writing is poor, if they have trouble following your lectures or classroom demonstrations, if they are reluctant to participate in class discussions and cannot articulate what they are learning or if they struggle to understand key concepts, it is highly likely that the heart of their struggle is difficulty with the vocabulary. To prevent these students from struggling in the first place, it is imperative that we help them develop the vocabulary they will need to think about the concepts we want them to learn.

Vocabulary is also necessary for comprehension. If your students are going to understand what is going on in the classroom, and if they are going to understand new concepts and acquire new skills in a content area, they must understand the vocabulary of that content area. Explicit vocabulary instruction helps prevent students from struggling by giving them a common language for learning and a way to express what they are learning. It helps students understand what is going on during instruction and allows them to express their own thinking clearly and concisely. Furthermore, when you and your students have a common language, it takes less time to understand and clear up students' misconceptions because students can explain the difficulty they're having and more easily understand your explanations.

Effective vocabulary instruction has been shown to increase student achievement by 33 percentile points (Marzano, Pickering, & Pollock, 2001). The key word here, though, is *effective*. Unfortunately, traditional vocabulary instruction—which usually involves students receiving a list of words, looking up the definition of those words, using the words in unrelated sentences, and perhaps taking a test on the words—is not only ineffective in helping students use the words in a meaningful way, but also particularly frustrating to struggling students. It asks them to memorize words without showing them how these words connect to and support their learning.

A better approach to vocabulary instruction involves previewing key vocabulary prior to the lesson. Do not focus on improving students' general vocabulary; just focus on those words they need in order to access the content. This way, students can develop familiarity with important vocabulary before the lesson begins and can more easily access the lesson instead of getting bogged down in trying to figure out what the new words mean.

Struggling students need multiple exposures to key vocabulary in order to retain it. It is not enough for them to learn the word once, especially if the word is taught at the beginning of the unit and out of context. We need to gradually shape the meaning of the word by helping students learn vocabulary both out of context at the beginning of the lesson and then again during the lesson.

Thus, the most effective vocabulary instruction does not simply rely on definitions. Instead, it asks students to interact with the words in a variety of ways. Not only should students be taught to define terms in their own words, they should be taught how to generate nonlinguistic representations of the words, such as pictures, charts, and diagrams. Creating an image of the word in addition to providing the word's definition creates another point of access for the brain, increasing the likelihood that the word's meaning can be retrieved from memory.

To preview vocabulary for your students, the first step is to decide what vocabulary is critical for students to understand if they are going to understand the new content. Don't create long word lists even if you are in a discipline with a lot of vocabulary. Instead focus on isolating the words that students must know and be able to use in order to learn the material at hand. Aim for a list of no more than 10 words for elementary students and no more than 20 words for middle and high school students. There may be other vocabulary that is important, and you may be able to teach it later, but the list you develop should contain those words that students absolutely need to know in order to reach mastery.

Next, determine how you will teach students these words. At this step, the key is to think about how students will use the word in the unit and let that drive your choice of instructional device. Think about how you want students to understand the word and select a vocabulary strategy that facilitates that understanding. Do you want students to grasp a concept? Use a word map or a Frayer model. Do you want students to understand how different concepts connect to each other? Use a concept map. Do you want students to be aware of the relationships among a list of words? Use a semantic feature analysis or a word sort. Do you want students to use the words to name things or processes? Use cue cards or diagrams.

After you have selected the strategy or strategies you will use to help students learn the new words, teach the new words approximately two days before you are ready to teach the new lesson or unit (one day before, if you are on a block schedule). Marzano (2003) suggests that you use a six-step strategy for introducing new vocabulary. Start by giving the students a brief description or explanation of the word. Do not rely on dictionary definitions, which are often inaccessible to students with limited vocabularies. Instead, describe what the word means and give students a brief example of the word. Next, provide students with a visual image of the word—show a picture of what the word describes, draw an example of the word, or share a symbol that illustrates it. The point is to help students develop familiarity with words before they encounter them as part of lesson content.

TAKE IT STEP BY STEP

Six Steps to Vocabulary Instruction

1. Students receive a brief, informal explanation, description, or demonstration of the term.
2. Students receive an imagery-based representation of the new term.
3. Students describe or explain the term in their own words.
4. Students create their own imagery-based representations for the term.
5. Students elaborate on the term by making connections with other words.
6. Over time, teachers ask students to add new information to their understanding of terms and delete or alter erroneous information. (Marzano, 2003)

Next, ask students to describe or explain the term in their own words. Here is where you can introduce a vocabulary tool, such as a Frayer model or a semantic map or cue cards. Students write down their own description or explanation and check it against yours for accuracy. Next, students construct their own image of the word. They can use a variation of the one you provided, or they can create one of their own. The key is to help students develop an imagery-based memory that will facilitate their remembering the word.

Then, ask students to make connections that help them expand their understanding of the term. Again, the vocabulary tool you use can facilitate this step. Students might compare the new word to a word they know already, make connections between all the new terms presented, or elaborate on the words by thinking up examples and non-examples of each. This step helps deepen students' understanding of the term and makes it more likely that they will remember the term when it shows up during the lesson.

At the beginning of your unit, remind students of the words they have learned through a short review session or by using one of the activating strategies we've mentioned. In this way you help prime students for learning the lesson. And because you have used a vocabulary strategy that helps build meaning beyond simply providing the definition, students can use the tool you have chosen as a "cheat sheet" throughout the lesson to help remind themselves of what the word means and how it should be used. Then, as the unit continues, take time to review the key terms and build meaning for students by showing them how each term is used within the context of the lesson.

Keep in mind that the initial instruction in vocabulary does not have to be particularly deep. You are looking to expose students to the word ahead of time so that they will be more likely to understand the lessons to come. As Marzano (2003) puts it, "A surface level knowledge of terms that form the basis for general understanding of a subject area is sufficient to provide students with a solid platform on which they can build more sophisticated understanding" (p. 58). Just exposing your students to key vocabulary ahead of time can dramatically accelerate their learning and prevent confusion later in the lesson.

Think about an upcoming lesson and use the **Vocabulary Planning Worksheet** on pages 40–41 to guide your selection of the vocabulary you will preview and the strategy you will use to preview it.

THINK ABOUT . . .

What is the key vocabulary for your upcoming unit? How will you expose your students to key vocabulary ahead of time?

Vocabulary Planning Worksheet

Key Concept:	
1. What are the **nouns** in the key concept statement? Do students know the meaning of these words?	
2. What words will students need to use and understand in order to **discuss or write about the key concept?** Do students know these words already?	
3. What **key words will you use in your class lectures and demonstrations** that students will need to understand in order to follow along?	
4. Will students be reading a text? What **words are used frequently in the text** that students will need to understand if they are going to understand the text?	
5. Referring to the **Anticipating Confusion Worksheet** on page 22, **what key words will students need to know** in order to understand this concept? What other words will confuse students if they do not fully understand their meaning?	

6. Take a look at the words you have written down so far. **What do these words have in common?** Do they name things? Processes? Related concepts or skills? Do they connect in some way? Do they contain similar semantic features?	
7. **Prioritize and group the words in order to select those that are most important to teach.** (Remember to choose no more than 10 words for elementary students and no more than 20 words for middle and high school students.)	
8. Think about how students will best learn the words and how you need them to use the words within the context of the class. Then **choose a strategy or a few strategies that will help students build a basic understanding of the words** before the lesson.	

YOUR TURN

Acquire: Familiarize yourself with the various vocabulary tools such as the Frayer model, cue cards, and semantic mapping. Experiment with these strategies in your classroom, and make note of which strategies seem to work best with your students, the type of vocabulary you use in your grade level or subject, and your own comfort level as a teacher.

Apply: Think about an upcoming lesson, select 5–10 words to preview, and use this entire process with your students. Make note of what worked, what didn't work, and what you would do differently next time. Slowly begin to integrate this process into your practice.

Assimilate: Think about how you currently teach vocabulary, and look for ways to add elements of the process presented here to your current practice. Begin to integrate more opportunities for students to create visual representations of the words they are learning, and shift when you teach the words so that you are previewing vocabulary prior to the lesson.

Adapt: Think about ways that you can refine both the timing of this strategy and the steps in the process so that they fit into your current practice. Also look for ways you could provide students who need additional support with other opportunities to increase their academic vocabulary outside class.

Providing Advance Organizers

For too many students, what they are doing in class and why they are doing it is a great big secret. When they are not let in on this secret, they cannot understand how what they are learning connects and are often lost during the unit. Thus, it is vital that we frame the learning for students. One way to do this is to provide them with advance organizers to preview what they will be learning.

You can use any kind of graphic organizer you like for this purpose, but the goal is to make clear to students the key vocabulary, concepts, and skills they will be learning in the unit and how each of these relates to the other and to what they have learned already. By showing students a graphic representation of where they are headed in the unit or lesson, you can help them see how all the lesson parts fit together and give them a clear understanding of what will be expected of them in the unit.

Once you have selected an appropriate advance organizer, share it with students one or two days prior to the lesson and walk them through it. Explain to them how the organizer is structured and how they can use it to help keep their learning organized. Practice the structure with them so that they are clear on how to use it. Then post it in the class so that students can refer to it throughout the unit. You should also refer to the advance organizer yourself as you progress through the unit. Don't hesitate to literally point out to students where you are so that they can see how what you are doing on any particular day will move them toward mastery. At the end of the lesson, advance organizers can also serve as a review tool for students as they prepare for final assessments.

On pages 44–45, you'll find an illustration of how both a 3rd grade teacher and a 10th grade language arts teacher might complete an advance organizer for a unit on persuasive writing. After you review these, move on to the **Advance Organizer Worksheet** on page 46 and start developing your own, referring back to the four worksheets you have completed so far. Make sure that you state both the key concept and the various content and contexts in "kid-friendly" language so that your students can easily follow the advance organizer as they work through the unit.

When you have completed that activity, think about an upcoming unit and use the **Acceleration Planning Worksheet** on pages 47–48 to plan how you will accelerate your students so that they will be prepared to be successful.

Effective acceleration is key to helping students get ready to learn. Because it cuts down on students' frustration and fear by preparing them for what is coming, it is a powerful way to head off trouble before it begins. By helping students develop the prerequisite skills they need for an upcoming unit and allowing them to become comfortable using these skills before they "need" them, you can set students up to learn successfully, increase their motivation to learn, and make their learning much more meaningful.

Sample Advance Organizer, 10th Grade English

Key Concept

A writer persuades his or her audience by three means: ethos, logos, and pathos.

Content

Ethos: A writer's character can be used to persuade an audience. The way that arguments and appeals are structured affects persuasiveness.	Logos: Appeals to logic can persuade an audience and address its concerns. The evidence a writer selects to support an argument affects persuasiveness.	Pathos: Emotional appeals can help engage the audience and advance an argument.	Rhetorical Grammar: Elements like grammar, punctuation, and vocabulary affect the writer's ability to persuade.

Context

• Read pp. 229–238 • Ethos exercise on p. 238 • Ethos analysis chart • Frayer model	• Read pp. 238–245 • Exercise on p. 245 • Induction/deduction chart • Frayer model	• Read pp. 246–259 • Pathos analysis exercises • Frayer model	• Sentence variety • Skills labs • Peer editing • Analyzing the rubric

Culminating Activity: Write a persuasive essay.

Vocabulary

ethos appeals character speaker	logos logical fallacy denotation deduction induction antithesis	pathos connotation alliteration	diction

Sample Advance Organizer, 3rd Grade

Key Concept
The choices I make in my writing can influence my readers' opinions.

Content		
The way I state my opinion can persuade my reader to accept my opinion.	The supporting details I use can persuade my reader to accept my opinion.	The way I organize information can persuade my reader to accept my opinion.

Context		
• Read "The Bicycle" and discuss in reading groups using discussion guides. • State Your Opinion! worksheet • Writing a thesis statement	• Mini-lesson on selecting supporting details • Writing a topic sentence • Writer's workshop on supporting a topic sentence with supporting details • Writer's group peer review	• Mini-lesson transition words • First, second, third… worksheet • Writer's group peer exchange

Final Activity: Create a persuasive essay in response to the story "The Bicycle."

Vocabulary		
opinion persuasion thesis statement	supporting details topic sentence	transition words organization

Advance Organizer Worksheet

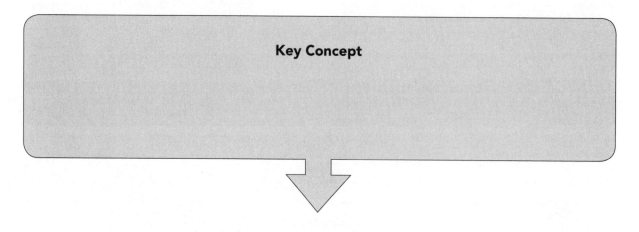

Content			
Context			
Vocabulary			

Acceleration Planning Worksheet

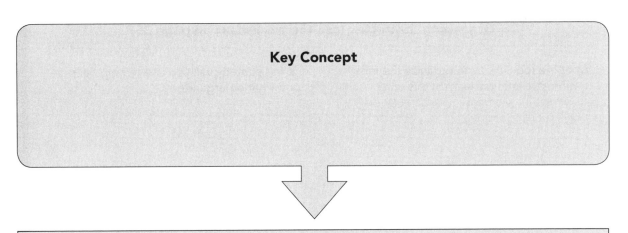

Activating or Creating Background Knowledge (use the worksheet on page 29)	
What background knowledge is required in order for students to understand the key concept?	How will you activate or create that background knowledge?

Advance Organizers (use the worksheet on page 46)	
How is your unit organized?	How will you graphically represent the upcoming content and the relationship among its concepts?

Organizing Strategies (use the worksheet on page 35)

What is a logical way to organize the information students will learn in this unit?	What strategy will you use to help keep information organized?

Vocabulary (use the worksheets on pages 40–41)

What is the key vocabulary students will need to understand in order to understand this unit?	How will you help students learn these words out of context?

YOUR TURN

Acquire: Select a relevant strategy from each of the four acceleration categories (activating/creating background knowledge, advance organizers, organizing strategies, and vocabulary). Try them out in an upcoming lesson and see how they affect students' ability to engage in that lesson.

Apply: Select an upcoming unit. Plan how you will accelerate students for that unit and implement the strategies with your students. Pay attention to how the students perform, and compare their performance to their performance in your last unit. What differences do you notice?

Assimilate: In addition to implementing the acceleration strategies in an upcoming unit, use acceleration to help prepare students ahead of time to be successful on summative assessments. Preview the summative assessment for that unit, and select applicable strategies to prepare students to show mastery on that assessment. Teach these strategies to students prior to the summative assessment. For example, if the test has a short-answer section, teach students to organize short-answer responses using a graphic organizer.

Adapt: Use pre-assessment to determine specific areas in which students require acceleration, and try using flexible grouping to target students requiring each type of acceleration while also offering extension activities for students who do not require acceleration.

YES, BUT...

It seems like you're recommending activating and creating prior knowledge for all of my students, but some students in my class are already well equipped to learn and ready to jump right in.

All students benefit from activating prior knowledge; it is a sound instructional practice that is already commonplace in many classrooms. Even if students have past experience with a topic, it never hurts to provide some reminders and context as they begin. Just think about how you routinely use this strategy in your daily life—making dinner, for example. Even when you're preparing a dish you've made before, you probably glance back over the list of ingredients or remind yourself of the cooking time. Or if you're traveling to a relatively familiar city, it never hurts to remind yourself of which exit to take or to jot down the addresses of places you'd like to visit.

Once you have conducted an activation activity with your students, you should begin to see which of them lack knowledge, have gaps in their knowledge, or are holding on to misconceptions. This provides a perfect opportunity to provide some customized instruction in your classroom. Perhaps while struggling students watch a video preview or work through an introductory text with you, students who are well prepared can work on an activity that extends or introduces a new level of complexity to the topic.

For example, let's say a middle school science teacher is preparing to introduce the digestive system. Fifteen of her 27 students have gaps in their knowledge and require previewing and acceleration. The remaining 12 students already have a good grasp of the basics of the digestive system and would find the previewing and acceleration boring or repetitive. While the teacher meets with the group of 15 students to show a short video and preview vocabulary, the group of 12 might work together to do an online tutorial about digestive diseases and disorders, read a higher-level article written for high school or college anatomy and physiology students about digestion, or do independent research on specific parts of the digestive system about which they could serve as experts during regular instruction.

Making sure that all your students are prepared for learning makes it more likely that they will all learn successfully.

Supporting Students
During Instruction

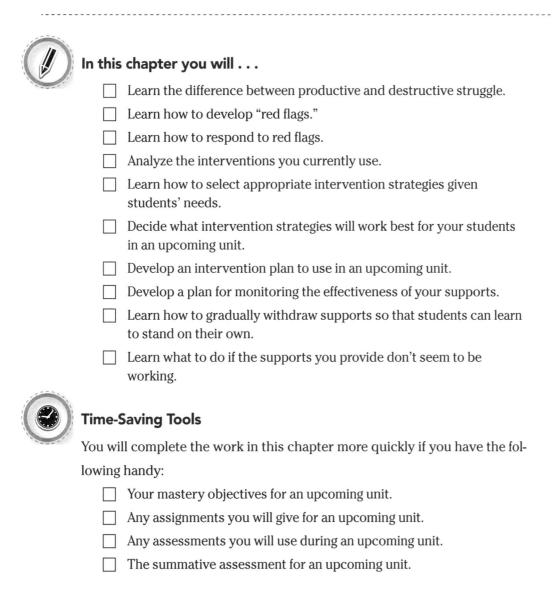

In this chapter you will . . .

- [ ] Learn the difference between productive and destructive struggle.
- [ ] Learn how to develop "red flags."
- [ ] Learn how to respond to red flags.
- [ ] Analyze the interventions you currently use.
- [ ] Learn how to select appropriate intervention strategies given students' needs.
- [ ] Decide what intervention strategies will work best for your students in an upcoming unit.
- [ ] Develop an intervention plan to use in an upcoming unit.
- [ ] Develop a plan for monitoring the effectiveness of your supports.
- [ ] Learn how to gradually withdraw supports so that students can learn to stand on their own.
- [ ] Learn what to do if the supports you provide don't seem to be working.

Time-Saving Tools

You will complete the work in this chapter more quickly if you have the following handy:

- [ ] Your mastery objectives for an upcoming unit.
- [ ] Any assignments you will give for an upcoming unit.
- [ ] Any assessments you will use during an upcoming unit.
- [ ] The summative assessment for an upcoming unit.

You have prepared your students for learning and set them up to be successful, but what happens if they still struggle? How will you help those students who falter during instruction?

Have you ever driven to an unfamiliar destination and realized far too late that you made a wrong turn or missed an important landmark? It's great when directions to a new spot include specifics like, "If you get to the red barn, you've gone too far" or "The turn is easy to miss, but it's coming up right after the gas station." A quick U-turn feels a lot better than realizing you've driven 45 minutes in the wrong direction. The same is true for your students. It is much more frustrating to get so lost in class that reaching mastery seems almost impossible. How much better would it be for struggling students if they could make a quick U-turn and get back on track?

So far, you have anticipated and prepared for points in the lesson where students might struggle, and you have provided students with strategies and support structures to prevent as much confusion and difficulty as possible. These supports help students successfully grapple with the learning tasks they face and build their confidence and ability so that they can reach the mastery threshold. Taking these steps will prevent most students in your class from faltering during the lesson, but there will be some students who, in spite of your preparation, will still struggle during the lesson, either because they are having difficulty with the material or because they are not putting forth the effort to learn.

In this chapter, we will focus on how to support students during instruction and how to address difficulty right away. You will learn the difference between productive and destructive struggle, learn how to create a plan that will help you recognize early on when students need intervention, and review a number of ways to respond to students' struggles quickly, efficiently, and systematically.

Why Students Struggle During a Lesson

There are a variety of reasons students struggle during the lesson. Some struggle because they don't understand and cannot retain the concepts you are teaching. Others need more time to master the new concepts. Students learn at different rates, and some students simply require more opportunities to practice what they are learning in order to "get it."

There are also students who struggle because they do not have the skills they need to navigate the learning context you have chosen. For instance, you may decide that your students will learn about shadows and eclipses by reading a chapter in the textbook. Students who have limited reading skills, ineffective note-taking skills, or poor time management may have a difficult time understanding shadows—not because the concept itself is too complex but because they do not have the skills they need to learn about shadows in the context of reading the textbook.

Finally, there are students who struggle because they do not put forth the effort necessary to work through the challenges of learning. Many who fall into this category do not understand the concepts of your course but use distracting or annoying behaviors to cover up this fact. Others simply opt out of the learning process altogether by skipping class or not turning in their work.

Productive Versus Destructive Struggle

The point of support and intervention is not to eliminate all struggle for students. Some struggle in learning is good, but there is a key distinction to be made between productive struggle and destructive struggle. *Productive struggle* allows students the space to grapple with information and come up with the solution for themselves. It develops resilience and persistence and helps students refine their own strategies for learning. In productive struggle, there is a light at the end of the tunnel; learning goals not only are clear but also seem achievable. Although students face difficulty, they grasp the point of the obstacles they face and believe that they will overcome these obstacles in the end.

Destructive struggle is different. Students cannot see how the difficulty or confusion they're experiencing will lead to any beneficial outcome. Learning goals seem unclear, even impossible. These students feel like their efforts are in vain, and they get frustrated and give up.

Before you intervene with students, you need to determine whether their struggle is productive or destructive. If students are struggling but their struggle is yielding results, then they do not need an intervention. Monitor their efforts to make sure it remains productive, but as long as they are making progress, allow them to continue to grapple with the material. However, if students are struggling and not seeing any benefit, if you see they are going nowhere and becoming hopelessly frustrated, you will need to intervene immediately. And in order to intervene immediately, you need to have a plan.

CHECKPOINT SUMMARY

Destructive Struggle	Productive Struggle
Leads to frustration	Leads to understanding
Makes learning goals feel hazy and out of reach and further effort seem pointless	Makes learning goals feel attainable and effort seem worthwhile
Feels fruitless	Yields results
Leaves students feeling abandoned and on their own	Leads students to feelings of empowerment and efficacy
Creates a sense of inadequacy	Creates a sense of hope

Intervention Development and Delivery

There are five steps to creating and implementing an effective intervention plan. We will look at each step in turn, and then you'll put all the steps together to establish your own intervention cycle.

TAKE IT STEP BY STEP

How to Develop and Deliver an Intervention Plan

1. Identify mastery thresholds.
2. Establish "red flags."
3. Develop ongoing assessment measures to identify red flags.
4. Select appropriate interventions.
5. Monitor the effectiveness of each intervention.

Step 1: Identify Mastery Thresholds

Mastery is not a single point of success; it is a range of successful behaviors. We certainly would like for every student to master 100 percent of the content, but a student who masters 80 percent of it is still successful. This student probably has the essential skills she needs to move on to the next unit or next grade level as well as the functional foundation necessary to grasp the more complex concepts coming her way. We would probably say that this student, at 80 percent, has achieved baseline or "entry level" mastery. Having crossed over this mastery threshold, she will now go on to greater success.

This focus on baselines may seem counterintuitive, especially because we so often hear about setting high standards and providing challenging instruction. Indeed, many students will *exceed* mastery and can be challenged through differentiated learning opportunities. But when you have to make instructional decisions about how to allocate time and resources and about how and when to intervene with struggling students, it is important to identify a baseline measure of mastery so that you can tell when students are falling into destructive struggle and require additional support.

Where threshold or baseline mastery lies is determined by you, the teacher, and the way you determine it is by analyzing what your standards and curriculum say students need to know and deciding how well they need to know it. Does earning a *C* on an assignment show mastery of the material? Can students miss more than two assignments during a marking period and still successfully master the course's standards? If a student misses more than three problems on a quiz, does that student understand the material? Can a student take sketchy notes and still be prepared for the test? What constitutes a solid working knowledge of the material? What is the level that all students must achieve in order to master the material?

THINK ABOUT . . .

What are some of your current mastery thresholds? How can you tell when students have moved from "almost got it" to "got it"?

YOUR TURN

Acquire: Start by establishing mastery thresholds for grades students earn. What is the lowest grade a student can earn on your next quiz or test and still be demonstrating mastery of the material? What is the lowest cumulative grade students can earn in your class and still demonstrate they are mastering the standards of your course?

Apply: Think about an upcoming unit. Use your curriculum guide as well as your own idea of what student success should look like to establish mastery thresholds for each assignment, quiz, and test you plan to use.

Assimilate: Think about your current mastery thresholds and look for gaps. What other mastery thresholds do you need to establish that will help you develop a fuller picture of students' mastery?

Adapt: Look beyond mastery thresholds that are strictly tied to academic achievement, and think about those behaviors students might demonstrate that tell you that they are or are not getting it. Establish mastery thresholds for academically related student behaviors that are implied by the curriculum, such as participation, note taking, study habits, and work completion.

Step 2: Establish "Red Flags"

"Red flags" are early-warning signals that a student is headed for destructive struggle. Once you establish a baseline for mastery, any time a student's performance falls below that baseline, that student has triggered a "red flag." For instance, if you decide that the baseline for mastery in your course is that students maintain a cumulative average of 80 percent, any time a student's grade point average falls below 80 percent, that student has triggered a red flag. If your mastery threshold is that students miss no more than five problems on their homework assignment, then a student who misses six problems has triggered a red flag. Once a student triggers a red flag, he or she immediately goes into the intervention cycle.

Red flags are useful for a number of reasons. Think back to your days as a student. Surely there were times when you sat in class feeling confused, overwhelmed, or underprepared. You probably weren't thinking *Gee, I hope the teacher calls on me in front of everyone or gives a pop quiz right now so she'll know I'm struggling and can intervene!* It's human nature to try to cover up what we don't know, hope we don't get called on, attempt to blend into the background, or scramble to catch up. Students who are truly overwhelmed and struggling often develop a broad range of coping behaviors to mask their confusion: becoming the class clown, developing an "out of it" persona, or becoming disruptive, just to name a few. Although most teachers can recognize these behaviors as coping strategies in retrospect, it's easy to get caught up in responding to and dealing with these behaviors and leave the confusion that perpetuates the behaviors unaddressed. Having red flags in place helps ensure objective, predictable triggers that denote academic issues and require an academic—not a behavioral—response. Teachers can approach these students calmly, with data in hand and an intervention to address student needs at the ready.

Red flags also help a teacher intervene earlier. Traditionally, intervention may come after a student has missed deadlines, failed a test, or not turned in an important assignment. But most of us can look at student data at the end of the semester and pinpoint the moment that student started to take a turn for the worse. Red flags call your attention to students' difficulties when students first begin to slip, before they have fallen significantly behind, and while they are still resilient rather than mired in failure.

Red flags are objective. They identify students who need intervention based on data rather than a teacher's idea of who is "needy" or a low performer. The fact is, kids we consider to be "smart"—and who consider *themselves* to be smart—often struggle with complex and multipart assignments, especially as they advance into late elementary and middle school. These students are particularly underprepared to ask for help and are likely to feel embarrassed about their struggle because they lack prior experience with academic difficulty. Compounding this problem is that they often give the appearance of "getting it"; they engage in class, they complete homework, and they demonstrate positive learning behaviors. That's why both we and these "smart kids" can be truly caught off guard when they miss the mark on an important assessment. The red flag system provides a fail-safe.

Finally, red flags help a teacher be more efficient. You can target the right kids and get them what they, specifically, need in order to meet the requirements of the task. You don't waste your time and their time applying random and general supports that may or may not address their needs. For example, if a student is having trouble converting fractions to decimals, it may be helpful to enroll him in the after-school math tutoring club, but this action won't directly address the issue he's having right now, which is converting fractions to decimals.

As Buffum, Mattos, and Weber (2009) remind us, "All too often, schools create broadly focused interventions, grouping struggling students together by the common symptom of failure rather than by the cause of their difficulties" (p. 65). Teachers who design and use red flags specifically linked to mastery thresholds in their own classrooms instead of looking for big symptoms with big solutions (e.g., *Peter doesn't do his homework, so let's have him work with an after-school tutor and mentor*) are able to bring a diagnostic element to their interventions. While Peter very well may benefit from working with a tutor and mentor, by setting and using red flags, his teacher will also know that Peter didn't turn in his homework because he had trouble making sense of the directions. With this knowledge, the teacher can provide a discreet, targeted intervention to be sure that Peter knows what he is supposed to do on the next homework assignment.

There are four cardinal rules for establishing red flags.

- ***Red flags should be unambiguous.*** You don't want to have to debate with yourself or with a student whether he or she has triggered a red flag. You want a clear signal that a student is falling below mastery.

- ***Red flags should be hard to ignore.*** You don't want to have to go hunting for red flags. You don't have time for that. Establish red flags that are easy to recognize and hard to miss.

- ***Red flags should trigger action.*** Once you see a red flag, you shouldn't have to figure out what to do about it. The moment a student triggers a red flag, you must be ready to apply an intervention. The longer you wait to respond, the further off-track that student is likely to be, and the more likely it is that his struggle will turn destructive.

- ***Red flags should be focused on academic concerns, not student behaviors.*** It may be a problem that students are talking in class and (therefore) not completing their work on time, but this talking is a behavior. It needs to be addressed outside your academic intervention plan, which must be tightly focused on helping students get back on track in terms of their comprehension and achievement. If you want students to invest in academic interventions, you must do everything you can to ensure that they do not perceive these interventions as punitive. Separating academic interventions from discipline or behavior management is half that battle.

THINK ABOUT . . .

Take a moment now to jot down some of the methods you currently use to determine that a student is struggling. What are some of the signals that let you know that students are falling below mastery? What are some signals that you have missed in the past?

YOUR TURN

Acquire: Pay attention to your students over the next two weeks. What signals do they give that let you know that they are beginning to struggle? Keep a list of these signals as a starting point for developing your own red flags.

Apply: Start identifying red flags that signal when your students are headed for trouble. Separate out those red flags that are strictly behavioral from those that are purely academic.

Assimilate: Think about the red flags you currently use to tip you off that students are headed for trouble. Look for gaps in your warning system, and identify additional red flags you can use.

Adapt: In addition to refining your own red flag list, create a list of red flags that signal other academic shifts your students make during a lesson. How can you tell when students are no longer struggling, for example? How can you tell that students are bored and ready to move on?

Step 3: Develop Ongoing Assessment Measures to Identify Red Flags

All teachers have ways of knowing which of their students aren't getting it. Some rely on data collection and analysis; others say they can just see it in the eyes of the students who don't understand. But these strategies, on their own, can lead teachers to overlook students who are lagging behind until those students are in serious academic trouble.

Thus the next step is to develop assessments to administer during instruction that will alert you when students trigger a red flag. These can be informal or formal: anything that lets you know how students are progressing toward mastery, from a quick check to make sure everyone is following the lesson to small quizzes, homework assignments, and performance tasks.

Be careful, however, not to rely solely on cursory checking devices such as "thumbs up" or asking a generalized, "Everybody understand?" Assessment techniques like these put the responsibility for recognizing or acknowledging confusion on the student. Instead we recommend strategies that are little more "meaty": small quizzes, homework assignments, and performance tasks that give you more specific information about how close students are to the mastery threshold and yield data you can more easily use in a formative way to guide instructional responses.

What mechanisms do you already have in place to track students' progress during the course of instruction? You don't have to create new ways of checking for understanding; it's perfectly fine to stick with the assessment strategies you are currently employing provided that you approach these strategies with a new eye for red flags. For instance, you currently grade papers and record students' progress, but now that you have identified what your red flags are, you will look for these red flags as you go about your normal grading, and you will respond to these red flags immediately.

Collect assessment data at regular intervals throughout a unit to stay abreast of student progress and identify those students whose progress is inadequate. Once you have administered the assessment, scan the overall data for performances that have triggered a red flag. These red flags will tell you which students are teetering on the edge of destructive struggle and in need of a quick and minimal intervention to guide them back to productive struggle and which students are well into the zone of destructive struggle and in need of more intense intervention. Students whose assessment results do not trigger a red flag are probably struggling productively, meaning that you can continue with the general supports you have in place.

YES, BUT . . .

All this assessment sounds like an awful lot of grading.

It's all in the timing. Yes, it does require a front-end investment of time in the evaluation of student work. But collecting and analyzing assessment data allow a teacher to identify and redirect students headed for failure—students who might otherwise give up on the process, never submit an essay, or turn in a paper that is way off the mark. By the time this teacher reads the final essays, she can be certain that the underlying structure for a successful essay is in place. What this means is that there will be very few failing essays by students who truly are in need of remediation and that these few will already have benefited from progressively intensive interventions along the way. It means that students who struggled along the way can be confident they are achieving mastery and that they won't find out too late that their grade in the course is unsalvageable.

In short, investing time in evaluation up front saves you time in the end. You cut down on your frustration and the frustrations your students' experience as you establish not just keener methods for locating students before they are overwhelmed by failure but also a broader repertoire of ways to move these students toward mastery of the material.

THINK ABOUT . . .

What assessments do you currently use to measure student progress during a unit? What kind of information do they provide about your students' performance? How do you currently respond to this information?

YOUR TURN

Acquire: Start collecting different types of assessments and assessment strategies you can use to monitor your students' progress during instruction, and begin experimenting with them in a unit. Using the red flag list you are creating, look for ways that the assessments you use can identify students who are headed for difficulty.

Apply: Use your red flag list to identify those assessments and assessment strategies that will best reveal each of your red flags. For instance, if you have identified understanding key vocabulary as a red flag, give students a quick vocabulary quiz or ask students to use the vocabulary in a paragraph for homework to check that they understand it.

Assimilate: Look for ways to directly connect your current assessments and assessment strategies with your red flags. Review the assignments you are planning to use in an upcoming unit, and consider the additional formative assessment data they might generate.

Adapt: Share your red flags with students, and show students how to use formative assessment data to track their own progress and "raise their own red flags" to alert you that they need additional support.

So far, we have established mastery thresholds, established red flags, and developed assessment measures to help identify red flags. Before going any further, let's take these first three steps and look at how to begin developing an intervention cycle.

Let's say a 7th grade English teacher plans to ask students to write a five-paragraph persuasive essay supporting one side or the other of the debate over school uniforms. The teacher first establishes the mastery thresholds—the criteria students must meet in order to be successful. Then, rather than wait until the essay submission deadline to collect data on students' mastery of this objective and its associated skills, the teacher also creates a series of formative assessments and checkpoints to help ensure that students are making progress toward mastery. A student who does not show appropriate progress triggers a red flag. Take a look at the chart on the next page, which illustrates the red flags this teacher might establish. Then turn your focus to an upcoming unit you plan to teach, and use the **Establishing Red Flags Worksheet** on page 65 to begin identifying your red flags.

Step 4: Select Appropriate Interventions

It isn't enough to simply know that students are struggling. Red flags identify the symptoms of failure, but interventions address the root causes. Once you have established your mastery threshold, identified your red flags, and established your assessment measures, the next step is to select an intervention that will address the academic concerns signaled by the red flag and help students get quickly back on track.

Interventions are different from general support. Support provides structures that help students be successful. They are proactive where interventions are reactive and undertaken in direct response to a red flag. Support provides general tools that help students access and be successful with the curriculum. Interventions provide targeted tools to address a specific, identified concern.

CHECKPOINT SUMMARY

Support	Interventions
Proactive	Reactive
General	Specific
Provided for all students	Provided for specific students
Prevents destructive struggle	Corrects destructive struggle
Predictive	Diagnostic

The most effective interventions provide a temporary learning support, are available to students on an as-needed basis, and are removed when they are no longer necessary. They allow struggling learners to access the regular lesson when the lesson demands content and skills that have, so far, been outside their reach. They give students the extra help they need consistently and without interruption until they can develop the skills and knowledge they need to independently engage in and be

Sample Red Flag Planning: 7th Grade English

Mastery Threshold	Assessment Measure	Red Flag
Write an effective thesis statement that clearly indicates the paper's position on the debate.	Following the introductory lesson and initial research, students submit an index card with their thesis statements.	The teacher gives three types of scores. A thesis statement can earn a 3 (ready for the essay draft), a 2 (requires minimal revision), or a 1 (is not effective). Papers earning a 1 trigger the red flag for intervention.
Write three topic sentences for the body paragraphs that reinforce the position.\n\nGather appropriate evidence from research to support the topic sentences.	After the second research session, students complete a graphic organizer with the now revised and approved thesis statement, the topic sentence for each body paragraph, and a quote or passage to support each topic sentence highlighted in their research documents.	The teacher reviews the graphic organizers and offers feedback. If an organizer has more than one ineffective topic sentence or more than two ineffective or insufficient pieces of evidence, the organizer triggers a red flag for intervention.
Use embedded quotations to cite the research.\n\nUse parenthetical citation for each quotation.	Following the lesson on embedded quotations and parenthetical citation and homework to reinforce skills, the teacher gives a multiple-choice quiz in which students read an excerpt from a sample article and choose which sentences correctly use embedded quotations and parenthetical citation.	If a student misses more than 4 of the 10 questions, that score triggers a red flag for intervention.
Write an effective conclusion.	Two days before the essay is due, students use a rubric to peer-edit their drafts and then write their conclusion paragraphs. On the back of the paper, each student writes the position and three topic sentences.	The teacher reads the conclusions. If she cannot identify either the thesis statement or two or more of the reinforcing topic sentences, this outcome triggers a red flag for intervention.

Establishing Red Flags Worksheet

Mastery Threshold	Assessment Measure	Red Flag

successful with a learning task. Effect interventions don't solve students' problems; what they do is provide students with just enough help so that the students can solve their problems on their own.

Because interventions provide students with only the support they need to get back on track, they should be progressive in nature: starting off at the modest, "just enough help" level and escalating as student needs require. This approach is wise for a several reasons. First, you don't want to implement an intensive intervention when a lesser intervention would be just as effective. Doing so handicaps students and may even be demotivating. Second, sequencing interventions so that they progress from least intensive to most intensive gives you options for students who continue to struggle in spite of early interventions.

Think of progressive intervention like you do progressive behavior management. The first time a student is whispering to a neighbor in class, it's unlikely that you would send her straight to the principal's office, set up a parent conference, or assign a week of after-school detention. Instead, you would probably start with a reminder about the classroom rules, a quick conversation, or a minimal consequence. If the student's behavior issue escalates, so too will your response.

Progressive intervention follows the same logic. A student's quiz score may trigger a red flag because she was having a bad day, she cut her studying short to focus on work for another class, or she fell one point below the mastery threshold. So your first intervention might be to have the student spend 10 minutes with a peer tutor reviewing the material or making a set of flashcards with correct answers to use when studying for the next assessment. Perhaps all that's required is a conversation with the student to review the directions for the assignment or direct her to an online tutorial or study guide that will firm up her understanding of the material. If this level of intervention is sufficient, the student will return to productive struggle or succeed without further assistance.

As noted, one of the beauties of red flags both for teachers and for students is that red flags are objective. Students don't need to come up with excuses for their subpar performance, and teachers don't have to worry that they are misinterpreting cues or classroom clues regarding the student's motivation or ability. At the point at which a student triggers a red flag, the intervention is no longer optional.

However, as you design interventions, remind yourself not to create more work for yourself than is necessary. If a quick conversation or simple measure solves the problem, that's terrific. If the initial intervention is ineffective or that first conversation reveals that the student is truly lost, you will respond with more intensive intervention.

When you introduce an intervention, make sure that you tell students that it is a temporary tool and that eventually they will be expected to work without it. You want to manage their expectations and prevent them from getting too attached to the tool.

Next, explain to students why the tool works and how it can help them learn on their own. Show students how the support will help their struggle be more productive but be careful not to give students the impression that the intervention will prevent their struggling altogether. Doing so creates false expectations that the intervention will solve all their problems and will only add to students' frustrations once they find out that the intervention is not a magic bullet. Instead, explain to students how the intervention will help them struggle more productively. Discuss the pros and cons of the strategy and explain why the strategy works.

After students have tried the strategy, ask for their feedback on how it worked for them. Give them the space to revise and adjust the strategy to make it work better for them. Ask students to share how they have adjusted the strategy with their peers so that you create a classroom bank of strategies.

Types of Interventions

Over the next several pages, we describe several types of interventions you can use with students, progressing from the least intensive to the most intensive. This collection is by no means exhaustive; it simply gives you a few examples of the types of interventions you can use. We encourage you to add to it as you discover your own ways to provide additional support to your students throughout your lessons.

Student Conferences

Sometimes all you need to do to get students back on track is to meet with them quickly to find out why they are struggling. Perhaps they didn't understand something you explained in class; if so, intervention is a matter of walking students through the information again and clearing up their confusion. Maybe students are experiencing problems outside the classroom that are affecting their performance in class. Talking with them can help you figure out the best way to provide assistance.

Try to make your conferences as supportive as possible. Don't lecture a student about what he is not doing or tell a student that she just has to "work harder." Instead, listen to what they have to say and ask probing questions to help you and the students understand why they are struggling. Consider the types of questions you will ask in advance. Rather than, "Did you study for the test?" try, "How did you study for the test?" Rather than, "Did you read the directions for the essay?" try, "Looking back, which part of the directions was most confusing?" With these questions asked and answered, you and the student can come up with a plan for getting learning back on track.

Be sure to include accountability measures in your plan. For example, don't just agree that the student will come in for extra help later in the week. Discuss what the purpose of the help will be and what will happen if the student misses the appointment. Finally, reiterate your commitment to support the student, and identify any resources you can provide to help the student turn things around.

Feedback

We cannot emphasize enough the power of feedback. Given the right kind of feedback, struggling students can gauge how they are doing and determine what they need to do to get to mastery. It can help students quickly correct their mistakes, select a more effective learning strategy, and experience success before frustration sets in. In order to use feedback as an intervention strategy, keep the following guidelines in mind:

- Feedback should be frequent.
- Feedback should show students the kinds of mistakes they are making and help them understand where the error lies.
- Feedback should show students how to correct their mistakes.
- Feedback should show students how close they are to mastery.

For struggling students, establish a tighter feedback loop where they receive growth-oriented feedback throughout the learning process, not just at the end. Doing so will help students gauge whether they are on the right track and correct their mistakes early, before they reach the point of frustration.

Concrete Examples

Some students struggle with material because they find it too abstract. They need concrete examples to help them understand. That is because "we understand new things in the context of the things we know, and most of what we know is concrete" (Willingham, 2009, p. 1495).

Analogies are your friend here. The key to using analogies is to make sure they're based on something students already know or understand and to be explicit as to how the new item is related. For example, suppose we wanted to teach the concept of gravity and told the students to "think of an apple falling off a tree." Just saying this won't help students understand. We must explain how the new thing (gravity) is related to the familiar thing (the falling apple).

You can also make abstract information more concrete by stripping it of extraneous and possibly distracting detail. Highlight the critical features of the concept that you want students to understand and leave out the other features that, while nice to know, get in the way of students understanding the concept. For example, when a science teacher introduces the chemical concept of pH to students, although it might be interesting to explain how the dyes in litmus paper interact with liquid to indicate a solution's acidity or basicity, this information is likely to distract students who are struggling to acquire a fundamental understanding of the concept. Because the goal is to ensure students understand the difference between acidic and alkaline, it's better to simply explain what the changes in the litmus paper indicate; the mechanics of litmus paper can wait until another time.

Consider saving examples of student work from year to year. Sometimes when students need to create a poster, write an essay, write a script, or the like, it is useful to have some exemplars to share. The sample projects need not be *A*+ assignments or on precisely the same topic the student will attempt, but providing an example or a visual often clarifies students' thinking.

Graphic Organizers

Although graphic organizers are typically used as a general support you share with the entire class, they can also be used as an intervention for students who are struggling with organizing and retaining information. For instance, you can provide students with a partially completed graphic organizer to help them take notes during a lecture or when reading a text, or you can use a graphic organizer to give students the location of where information can be found in the text. For students who have difficulty reading a textbook chapter for homework, you can use anticipation guides to help them see the underlying organizational structure of the chapter and alert them to how the ideas in the chapter connect. You can even give them a clue sheet that helps them hunt for clues in the text that will help them answer questions about the material.

Graphic organizers are particularly helpful in calling students' attention to what's important. We know that students can only learn what they pay attention to. If your students are struggling because they are missing crucial information in their texts or they are not taking effective notes during class or they don't pick up the key content in class discussions, give them a graphic organizer that helps focus their attention on the most important information.

You may even wish to meet with students to go back over the notes they take with their graphic organizers, comparing what they wrote down to a set of teacher notes or effective sample notes from another student. Students who are ineffective note-takers have a hard time envisioning what useful notes look like; comparing their own work to stronger work can give them direction.

"Cheat Sheets" and Cues

Although the name implies otherwise, cheat sheets are great tools for helping struggling students keep up with the rest of the class. For example, if students have trouble remembering the steps for solving quadratic equations or looking at a slide under the microscope or writing a five-paragraph essay, give them a cheat sheet that lists the steps involved. As they are working, they can quickly consult their cheat sheet and get back on track. Or if students have a difficult time following your lecture or keeping up with your pace as they take notes during class, give them a copy of your overhead slides with space for notes. As students gradually develop their own competency, show them how to make their own "cheat sheets" to help them through an assignment.

Instead of distributing prepared cheat sheets, you might simply provide struggling students with verbal or written cues to help them keep up with the class or complete an assignment correctly. For example, you could cue students who are working along with a class demonstration by saying, "By the time I get out the digi-blocks, you should be at the bottom of page 2." Or you could tell students approximately how long a homework assignment should take. You could embed written reminders in your worksheets pointing students to places in the text where they can find the information they need in order to answer the question or clues about what strategy they should use to solve the problem.

Memory Strategies

Often students struggle with the content because they do not have the memory strategies they need to retain information. You'll recall from your Psych 101 courses that thinking critically involves both long-term memory, where most information is stored, and short-term or working memory, the repository of various bits of information you retrieve from long-term memory and manipulate to formulate thoughts, articulate ideas, and solve problems. Working memory has a very limited capacity. Most of us can only store about seven chunks of information. If we want to retain more information, we need to "chunk" it together, so that we can hold more information in our working memory. For an illustration, try to memorize the following string of letters: X, C, N, N, P, H, D, F, B, I, C, I, A, X. Perhaps with some practice, you could remember them all, but it would be a lot easier if you chunked them: X, CNN, PHD, FBI, CIA, X. Now remembering the string of letters is much easier.

The problem for many struggling students is that most information they encounter in school is like a string of random letters. They don't see the connections between ideas or information. And without seeing the connections, they have a harder time chunking information so that they can hold more of it in their working memory. What's more, sometimes these students are not good at storing information in long-term memory in an organized way, meaning that they also have trouble retrieving it when they need it.

Students who have difficulty with storing and retrieving information greatly benefit from being taught how to remember what they have learned. Memory strategies help students organize and store new information so that they can use it to attain understanding of a concept with which they are struggling. They can also show students how to "chunk" information so that they can hold more information in their working memory and use it to formulate solutions to problems and think critically.

The reason mnemonics are so effective for struggling students is that they provide a way to impose order on information that may seem arbitrary or confusing. In other words, mnemonics create cues that students can use to recall what they need to learn. Students can use the first-letter mnemonic method to create a word that will help them remember all the components in a category. Most of us learned the order of operations by remembering FOIL and the Great Lakes by remembering HOMES. When students need to remember those items in a particular order, the sentence method is helpful. There are many of us who still think "Every Good Boy Does Fine" when trying to read sheet music. You can also set what you are trying to remember to the tune of a familiar song. To this day, many parents still teach their children the alphabet by setting it to the familiar tune of "Twinkle, Twinkle, Little Star."

The key to memory strategies is creating connections and providing practice. When you select a memory strategy for students, try to think of ways they might connect what they are trying to remember to something that's already familiar to them. You want to help them make an abstract idea more concrete, more accessible. For example, when introducing students to new vocabulary, try drawing pictures or acting out a story or "commercial" for the word. When focusing them on new material, compare what you want them to understand to something they'll find familiar, such as how the layers of the earth's crust are similar to the layers of a lasagna. Search out songs or hand motions that create an auditory or physical connection to new ideas. Use pictures or characters to remind students of a concept—think of the old Schoolhouse Rock train rolling through "Conjunction Junction." Creating connections helps students build "hooks" and makes the new information stickier.

Once you have found a connection, the next step is to give students sufficient practice that will strengthen these connections in students' brains. Set aside practice time in class and clearly communicate the expectation that students will continue their practice at home.

Summarizing

Some students struggle because they do not understand what they have read or heard in class. These students need time to process what they have learned, and they need opportunities to check their own understanding. Summarizing helps students create a schema for remembering what they have learned and remember it longer. Studies have shown that when students talk about what they are learning, the odds that they remember what they have learned increase twofold (Thompson et al., 2005).

You can also have students write about what they learn as a summarizing strategy and as a way to help them clarify their own thinking. (You can review these pieces to check on students' understanding.) Be sure to distribute summarizing activities throughout the unit instead of reserving them for the end. Giving students the opportunity to process and reflect what they are learning leads to overall gains in understanding.

Summarizing is a great way to help students who misunderstand what they read for homework in the text or do not process what they have read. After assigning students homework, begin the class the following day by asking students to summarize what they read the night before and write down any questions. You can even ask students to write a summary using their notes if you want to emphasize the value of good note taking. Then students share what they wrote with a partner and fill in each other's summaries and attempt to answer their classmates' questions. Finally, the pairs raise any unanswered questions to the class during a brief class discussion of the homework.

To help students who have difficulty processing what they are learning during a lecture or a classroom demonstration or a film or the like, break the activity up into smaller chunks and give students opportunities to summarize what they are learning throughout.

"Break Glass" Strategies

We've all seen the signs, "When in an emergency, break the glass." Behind the glass is the tool we need to manage the emergency and save our lives. When struggling students get stuck and do not know how to work their way out of difficulty, they also need a "break glass" strategy they can use to manage the difficulty and keep from becoming frustrated and giving up. Maybe it is a process they memorize for steps to work their way out of a problem or a list of things to check when the answer does not turn out the right way. Perhaps it is an online discussion group where they can post their questions to their classmates or a one-time "phone a friend" pass they can use in class when they can't answer a question during a class discussion. Maybe you give them a literal red flag they can wave or place on their papers next to an item they don't understand to signal that they need help. Or maybe it's as simple as showing students how to use a classroom resource ahead of time so that they can access it when they get stuck. Giving students a way to work their way out of difficulty prevents frustration and builds students' confidence and resilience.

Tiered Homework Assignments

Tiered homework assignments allow students to get the extra practice they need at the level they need it. Think of doing homework like practicing tennis—if you always play against your 4-year-old cousin, you'll never get better because there's no opportunity to stretch. If you always play against someone who just won at Wimbledon, you'll never get better because you'll be overwhelmed. But if you play with someone who is just a little better than you are, your skills will rise as you work to meet this appropriate challenge.

If you usually ask your students to complete 20 or so problems for homework—and you spend your time during or after class grading this homework—consider creating tiered homework assignments. This strategy works best for homework that provides practice with concrete skills like math or science computation, grammar, foreign-language verb conjugations, and the like. In the last 10 minutes of class give a very short assessment (4–5 questions) that covers the content of that night's homework. Have students check their own work on the spot, collect and scan the work, and then tier your homework assignments to address a range of student needs:

- To students who answer all the questions correctly, give minimal practice and a challenge application or extension. These students clearly get it, so they can self-check with an answer key the next day.

- For students who miss a couple of problems, provide review and practice. They can self-check homework with an answer key and help one another or identify a few problems as a group for which they would like teacher assistance.

- For students missing nearly all the problems, provide homework that focuses on building understanding of the concept and includes a few practice problems related to each concept. Remember to keep the number or repetition of practice problems modest for this group so they don't become overwhelmed. Plan to devote the time the next day you would normally have spent checking homework with the whole class to providing reteaching to this group.

Modeling Thinking Strategies

Some struggling students need to see how to think through a problem first before they can begin to do it on their own. Thinking aloud makes thinking processes involved in solving problems clear to students.

Here is the way it works. Have students watch you work through a problem. As you work, say aloud what is going through your mind so that students can see your thinking process. For instance, let's say that your students still don't understand the thinking involved in solving for x in the following sample problem: $x + 9 = 12$. As you solve the problem in front of students, you might say something like this:

Hmmm. OK, so I need to solve for x. Let me see. How do I do that? OK, I know that I need to get x on one side of the equal sign and all the other numbers on the other side. So I need get the 9 from where it is now, on the left side, over to the right side. Well, since the 9 is a positive number, I can subtract it from both sides and that will get rid of it on the side with the x and put it on the other side of the equal sign. So that leaves me with x = 12 − 9. Right. So what is 12 − 9? It's 3. That leaves me with x = 3. OK, let me check to make sure I did this right. If x = 3, then 3 + 9 should equal 12. It does! Great! I did it right.

By modeling the thinking process involved in solving a problem, you can show students what the steps in the process look like in action. Thinking aloud not only helps you model the thought processes you want your students to adopt, it also shows students how to work their way out of difficulty.

Task Breakdowns

Some students struggle because they don't understand all of the steps involved in a process. Simply providing students with a list of the steps involved can help them keep track of the steps. Other times, students know the steps involved but are unclear how to complete one or more steps. Break those steps down into smaller parts or isolate the steps so that students can just focus on these and are not overwhelmed by the entire process. Next, give students plenty of practice with each step and, once they demonstrate proficiency, begin to bundle steps until they can seamlessly perform the entire process.

Mandatory Extra Help

Mandatory extra help, such as study halls, makeup sessions, or homework clubs, provide students with a quiet, structured environment in which they can make up missing work, get extra help on assignments, or complete current work. Students can get tutoring on concepts that they still don't understand or assistance as they work through their assignments. These sessions are best for students who have fallen behind, are not keeping up with their current work, or need additional supervision and support in order to complete their assignments effectively and on time.

Peer Tutoring

Many students find learning or practicing with a peer more accessible and less anxiety producing than working with a teacher all the time. Think about being a new driver.

Didn't it always seem easier to practice new skills with an older sibling or slightly more experienced driver than with the Driver's Ed teacher or a parent? In the same way, many struggling students enjoy working with a nonstruggling classmate to practice or review skills and may be more likely to ask honest questions and take risks when the teacher isn't directly involved. As long as the teacher provides the content and the overall directions for peer tutoring, it can be a powerful and valuable practice: one that also reinforces learning for the tutor and furthers positive classroom connections.

THINK ABOUT . . .

Which interventions on this list do you use already? What other interventions did you see that you might try using in an upcoming lesson or unit?

YOUR TURN

Acquire: Select one of the interventions in the preceding section to try in an upcoming unit. Keep notes on how well it worked and what you might do differently next time.

Apply: Select three related interventions from the preceding section to use in an upcoming unit. Start with the least intensive and move on to ones that are more intensive.

Assimilate: List all the interventions you use already, from the least intrusive one to the most intrusive. Select three interventions from the list in the preceding section to add to and round out your current list. Add these interventions to those you already offer your next unit.

Adapt: Take one or more of the interventions in the preceding section and adapt it to fit a particular student or an upcoming lesson.

GUIDELINES FOR INTERVENTION SELECTION

The key to effective interventions is to select the right response to each red flag. As you design interventions that best fit the requirements of your course, there are some guiding principles to keep in mind.

- ***Interventions should be designed to get students quickly back on track.*** Interventions, unlike general supports, are designed to address students' immediate needs and keep up with the learning taking place in the classroom. Students should be able to see the immediate usefulness of an intervention and understand how it will help them be more successful with the learning task at hand.

- ***Interventions should not be punitive.*** You do not want to punish students for struggling, even if they are struggling because of irresponsible behavior. You can address the behavior in another way. The point of an intervention is to help the student learn the information he has not learned and catch up. For instance, if students are struggling because they are not completing their homework, making them attend after-school detention to do a week's worth of homework may get the homework turned in, but it won't address the reasons why the student isn't turning in his homework in the first place. And just because a student completes his homework under those conditions does not mean that the student has learned what he didn't know before. Such an intervention is more focused on the student's behavior than it is on his learning. While you can and should promote the desired behavior for your classroom, be sure to design academic interventions that address the issue at hand. Perhaps the student needs instructions that are broken down or to repeat the instructions in his own words before beginning a new task. Maybe the student needs a tiered or scaffolded homework assignment. Look for academic interventions that work in tandem with your behavioral interventions.

- ***Interventions should be seamless and unobtrusive.*** They should not draw negative attention to students who are using them. They should be built into the structure of the classroom and ideally available to all students but mandatory for some.

- ***Interventions should be systematic.*** They should not leave students' access to them to chance or be administered in a random or haphazard way. Instead, they should be a vital, sequential part of the instructional program. As soon as a student triggers a red flag, that student should immediately get the appropriate intervention.

- ***Interventions should be temporary.*** Students should not be locked into an intervention cycle with no hope of escape. Interventions are designed to help students catch up and keep up with the rest of the class. After students have caught up, gradually withdraw the interventions and allow them to exit from the intervention cycle with the expectation that now that they have received their support, they will keep up with the rest of the class.

- ***Interventions should be minimal.*** They should provide just enough support so that students can be successful on their own. They should be sequenced so that they grow progressively more intensive as students demonstrate that they need more help.

- ***Interventions should be specific.*** They should address the problem signaled by the red flag, not all the student's academic challenges. For example, if a student is having trouble multiplying fractions because she doesn't know the 8s and 9s times tables, you don't need to reteach the foundations of multiplication. Instead, try giving her a copy of the 8s and 9s times tables and practice problems that use these calculations so she can learn this missing material. Once she has grown comfortable with the 8s and 9s, remove the support.

- ***Interventions should not be labor intensive.*** Many times we create interventions that require us to work harder than our students. Doing so prevents you from intervening with more than a few students at a time. Your interventions need to be scalable so that if several students are struggling at one time, you are able to intervene with each of these students without killing yourself in the process. Consider using online tutorials, simulations, or videos that can be accessed by many students. Coordinate review or study groups that require a single preparation but can impact many students. Provide practice activities that are self-guided or allow students to work with partners or teams.

THINK ABOUT . . .

How do your current interventions stack up against these criteria? How can you make your interventions more systematic and seamless? What are ways you can make the interventions you choose less labor intensive but still effective?

Sample Red Flags and Corresponding Interventions

You have spent some time thinking about the red flags in your class and reviewing and brainstorming possible interventions. Now it's time to start making connections between the two. Master teachers do an excellent job of choosing not just any intervention but *the right intervention* to help specific students. The more you practice interventions, the richer your repertoire will become, and the easier it will be to help your students. You will also be able to save any materials you find or create from unit to unit or year to year, making the intervention process less and less work for you.

As you consider the intervention, think of the process like putting out a fire. Let's say you're relaxing at home by a cozy fire when suddenly a spark leaps from the fireplace and the carpet begins to smolder. Drawing from what we've all learned about fire safety, here are a few things you could choose to do at the moment smoke begins to rise:

> a. Create a diagram of your home and teach your children safe escape routes.
> b. Install smoke alarms and check them routinely to make sure they work.
> c. Stop, drop, and roll.
> d. Grab the glass of water you're drinking and pour it on the smoldering carpet. Then carefully check the area to make sure the fire is out.

All of these are good fire safety practices, but only choice *d* is exactly right at this moment. As you begin designing red flags and interventions, you will build your skills at identifying the exact intervention that is right for the moment.

The figure on the next page shows some sample red flags and corresponding interventions. Consider these examples as you tackle the **Intervention Planning Worksheet** that follows, on page 81. It asks you to look again at the mastery thresholds you identified when completing page 65's Establishing Red Flags Worksheet and determine a corresponding intervention.

Step 5: Monitor the Effectiveness of Each Intervention

It's important to be systematic about intervention monitoring. Part of your planning must address how often you will check to see if students are making progress. What assessment measures will you use? Will you check students' GPA every two weeks to see if they are making progress? Are there certain homework assignments you will monitor over time to see if students are improving? Will you meet with students periodically to see how they are doing or work with them in small groups to monitor their growing understanding of a concept? Perhaps you will ask students to self-assess and report to you how helpful they find a particular intervention. Think about how you will

Sample Red Flags and Corresponding Progressive Interventions

Focus	Red Flags	Progressive Interventions
Student Grade Point Average	Grade point average of 79% or below at the first two-week checkpoint	– One-on-one conference to develop a plan to get back on track – Assigned online simulation or tutorial.
	Grade point average of 79% or below two consecutive times	– Mandatory attendance at twice-weekly homework help sessions during lunch – Call home
	Grade point average of 79% or below three consecutive times	– Conference attended by teacher, student, guidance counselor, and parent – Mandatory after-school tutoring
Summative Assessment Score	Test grade of 79% or below	– Mandatory makeup session and retake
	Missing the same types of problems on a test	– Study session to learn "break glass strategies" – Retake
	Failing a test	– Conference with teacher to review strategies – Retake
Classwork	Missing four or more problems on the worksheet	– "Cheat sheet" pointing students to the pages in the textbook they can go to for extra help on each problem
	Incomplete notes	– Note-taking graphic organizer or a partially filled-in graphic organizer
	Limited contributions to small-group or class discussion	– Conversation with teacher – Prediscussion organizer or "cheat sheet"
	Not starting on classwork right away after being given instructions	– Conversation with teacher – List of steps for getting started
	Not following instructions on classwork	– Classwork instructions checklist
Assessment Data Gathered During Instruction	Missing five or more problems on a quiz	– Mandatory reteaching and retake.
	Earning a 69% or below on a quiz	– Graphic organizer to help students take notes on the reading – Call home – Mandatory makeup session – Assigned online tutorial
Homework	Incomplete homework assignments	– Tiered homework assignments
	Not submitting homework or submitting largely incomplete homework	– Conversation with teacher and deadline for makeup – Tiered homework assignment
	Responding incorrectly to 25% or more of homework	– Peer tutoring session or reteaching during class, lunch, or study hall time – Independent review, such as online tutorial or review worksheet

Intervention Planning Worksheet

Red Flags What are your "red flags" in this unit? What will tell you that students are not being successful?	**Interventions** What corrective actions will help get students back on track?

know whether students are approaching the mastery threshold and, as you provide intervention, be mindful of whether the intervention you are using is actually working.

Even with intervention, students may not reach the mastery threshold right away. The key is to look to see if students are making better progress toward mastery than they were before you applied the intervention. Is the intervention making a difference in students' ability to access and understand the information? Can you document the gains they have made?

The goal of interventions is to get students quickly back on track. But what do you do when the interventions you have selected don't seem to be working?

Look at the Match Between Intervention and Need

First, you need to examine the intervention to see if it is really addressing the root cause for students' difficulty. Sometimes the intervention is not working because, while it may address a symptom of students' difficulty, it does not correct the underlying cause. For instance, say you give a student who demonstrated poor understanding of the textbook's chapter 4 content a vocabulary "cheat sheet" to use as she reads chapter 5. But if the root cause of her difficulty with the text is not vocabulary but that she doesn't have the effective note-taking strategies that will help her remember what she reads, the support you have provided will do nothing to help solve her problem.

You should also check to see that the intervention you provide does not create additional work for students. Let's take our student above. Suppose her trouble really is vocabulary. Giving her a "cheat sheet" requires her to take an additional step as she reads. Not only does she have to try to sustain her attention as she reads, she has to interrupt her reading process from time to time to refer to the cheat sheet. Thus, the support that was designed to make her reading process easier has actually made it more difficult.

So before moving to more intensive supports, check first to see if the intervention you have provided really addresses the student's needs. And make sure that the intervention is not creating unintended additional problems for the student.

Consider a More Intensive Intervention

Because you have sequenced your interventions so that they grow in intensity from the least intrusive to the most intensive, you can select a more intensive intervention for students for whom a lesser intervention does not seem to be working.

Sometimes, you don't need a more intensive intervention; you just need more time for a specific intervention to work. Some learning difficulties are easier to address; some are more difficult. You can't expect a quick fix every time. Also note that students may not need a more intensive intervention, just more frequent exposure to the current one. This is often a good approach if the student gains you are seeing are smaller than you'd like. For instance, let's say a student is able to complete writing assignments in response to a text when given an organizer to capture evidence while reading but falters when an organizer is not provided. You could consider providing organizers more frequently and helping the student create his own organizers once he is familiar with the strategy.

CONSIDER ADDITIONAL RESOURCES

Finally, determine whether you need to access other resources. Sometimes using red flags and interventions will signal to a teacher that there is an academic problem whose reach extends beyond this assignment, concept, or course. Particularly if you are working with younger students and students who are new to your school or district, you may begin to suspect that learning disabilities, limited English proficiency, health issues, neglect or abuse, or vision/hearing/speech deficiencies are contributing to a student's difficulties. While you should still offer classroom-based interventions, there is no need to go it alone when other specialists or resources in your building or district can help you to support a struggling child. In fact, armed with your data about specific red flags and interventions that have worked (or not), you will be well prepared to ensure your students are screened and supported appropriately.

Helping Students Exit the Intervention Cycle

The moment a student is back on track, as signaled by assessment data showing he or she has reached the mastery threshold, begin planning that student's exit from the intervention cycle.

Any supports you choose should be designed to be withdrawn as students develop more proficiency. In that way, you build students' own capacity to complete the work and understand key concepts without additional supports and help them learn to be successful on their own.

Think about what the support you have in place is intended to do. Are you helping students develop better organizational strategies or helping students understand key vocabulary? Are you helping students learn to read text independently or study more effectively? Remembering the purpose of the supports you provide helps you recognize when the support has met its purpose and can be safely removed.

There are several different ways to withdraw support gradually. You can decrease the amount of support you provide for students over time. If at the beginning of the year you provided the students with scaffolded graphic organizers to help them take notes in the text, over time you can provide them with less scaffolding and leave more space for them to provide notes on their own. Or if you have been providing students with "cheat sheets" to help them study, provide shorter cheat sheets as the year progresses.

Another way to gradually withdraw support is to increase the number of steps students must complete on their own. Perhaps you are accustomed to providing students feedback between each step in the process. As students become more proficient, you can provide feedback every two steps and then every four steps and so on so that students complete more of the work on their own. You can also bundle the steps in the process. If you have taken a concept or a process and broken it down into several steps, as students grow in their understanding, you can compact the process and reduce the number of steps.

You can also decrease the frequency of support. As students develop their proficiency, you can provide fewer after-school study sessions or take less time during class to preteach organizing strategies as students accumulate their own organizing strategies.

Let's say that you allow students to use their notes on a test. If you simply continue to do so for the entire year, students might come to depend on having access to their notes and may not learn the concepts as deeply as they need to. And they may have difficulty completing state tests, where notes are not allowed. If you suddenly prohibit students from using their notes when they have become accustomed to using them, you are setting them up for failure. The rule of thumb, with this and all support measures, is to withdraw it gradually. You might try this approach:

> Test 1: All notes are allowed.
> Test 2: Notes are allowed during the last half of the test period.
> Test 3: Notes are allowed during the last five minutes of the test period.
> Test 4: No notes allowed.

Here's another way:

Test 1: All notes are allowed

Test 2: Students can use one 8-1/2" × 11" sheet of notes.

Test 3: Students can use one 5" × 7" card of notes.

Test 4: No notes allowed.

And yet another way:

Test 1: All notes are allowed.

Test 2: Students create a class "cheat sheet" to use on the test, and all students may use this set of notes during the test.

Test 3: Students cannot use their notes but are allowed five minutes at the beginning of class to create a fresh set of test notes on a scratch sheet of paper; they can use these notes and no others during the test.

Test 4: No notes allowed.

When you first attempt to remove supports, some students will protest. They have become accustomed to having a certain level of support and will resist having to work without it. They may even show signs of struggle at first as they learn to work on their own. Resist the temptation to rush right back in with more support; allow them to struggle productively. At this point, your role is to remind students of the strategies you have taught them and coach them on how to apply these strategies to manage new challenges. You may even have to increase the amount of feedback you give them as they begin to do more and more on their own. It can be helpful to walk students back through the intervention process and the progress they've made. For example, you might ask a student to remember the red flag that led to intervention—a failed quiz, perhaps. Remind the student that, together, you discovered why he had failed that quiz—ineffective notes. Then recount the steps you took to address this skill deficiency—the partially completed graphic organizers you provided to support better note taking, the note reviews you did together, and the subsequent organizers that required the student to fill in more and more information independently. Show the student how he has built his skills in organizing information from lectures. Talk about how he might now succeed without your intervention. Could he create his own organizer? Use a note-taking technique he has practiced? Meet with a friend after class to review the notes? As you prepare to hand responsibility for learning back to the student, make sure he has a plan for accepting it.

YES, BUT . . .

These intervention strategies assume that students want the help. What do I do about students who refuse to be helped or who have given up altogether?

The first thing to do is to figure out why students are refusing your help. For many struggling students, extra help just seems like extra work. Make sure that the supports you suggest make the work more manageable for students, and show them how the supports you provide will help them get better results for the effort they expend. For other students, support seems like punishment, especially if it's only available during what they consider "their time": at lunch, after school, or on weekends. Find ways to provide students support during the school day. And then there are the students who have been caught in the cycle of failure for so long that they've given up. If you can't show these students how the supports you are suggesting will actually help them meet or exceed the standards, it's unlikely they will be willing to try them. You need to make your case clearly and work on helping them believe that the key to "getting smarter" is effective effort. Carol Dweck's 2006 book *Mindset* has some great strategies for helping students develop this growth mindset.

3

Supporting Students
After Instruction

In this chapter you will . . .

- [ ] Learn how to provide effective remediation.
- [ ] Learn how to conduct an error analysis to understand why students are still struggling.
- [ ] Learn how to select appropriate remediation strategies.
- [ ] Decide what remediation will work best for your students in an upcoming unit.
- [ ] Learn how to implement a reteaching and reassessing cycle that will help students master the material.
- [ ] Develop a remediation plan to use in an upcoming unit.

Time-Saving Tools

You will complete the work in this chapter more quickly if you have the following handy:

- [ ] Any assignments you will give for an upcoming unit.
- [ ] Any assessments you will use during an upcoming unit.
- [ ] The summative assessment for an upcoming unit.

You've prepared students to be successful with general supports, and you have provided targeted intervention to students who struggle during the lesson to quickly get them back on track. What do you do about students who still don't get it?

The acceleration and intervention strategies presented so far in this guide provide teachers with a way to significantly increase the number of students who will meet mastery thresholds. However, even after you have supported students prior to the lesson or unit and have provided more targeted intervention for students during the learning, you may have a handful of students who struggle with parts of the material and, as the unit draws to a close and the summative assessment approaches, still do not understand key concepts or still cannot demonstrate mastery of required skills.

There are numerous reasons these students may continue to struggle. They may have gaps in their learning that make it hard for them to understand key concepts, even with support. Some may be having trouble applying the strategies you've worked on with them. Others may be having difficulty sustaining attention or motivation or may have misconceptions about the subject that persist and interfere with their learning. Some students may be committed to distracting behaviors that interfere with their learning, and others may simply be deliberately avoiding learning altogether. Some of these reasons are purely academic and can be addressed by remediation alone.

Others are behaviors that compound academic difficulty and need to be addressed both by remediation and by behavior management techniques outlined in other guides in this series.

Regardless of the reason these students have yet to be successful, it is important to provide them with remediation so that they have another chance to reach the mastery threshold prior to the summative assessment.

✓ CHECKPOINT SUMMARY

Acceleration	Intervention	Remediation
All students	Some students	Few students
Before the lesson or unit	During the lesson or unit	Toward the end of the lesson or unit
Prepares students for learning	Supports students as they learn	Fills in the gaps of students' learning prior to the summative assessment
Conducted during class	Conducted during and (sometimes) before and after class	Before or after class and at home

Remediation

Remediation is an opportunity to provide additional support to those students who still do not understand key concepts in spite of earlier attempts to support them before and during the lesson. With remediation, these students have another chance at learning prior to a summative assessment.

Remediation is different from the other supports we've discussed so far. While acceleration and intervention are offered before and as students are learning for the purpose of facilitating that learning, remediation is offered *after* students were supposed to have mastered the content. And while most of the supports we have discussed so far happen inside the classroom during the regular lesson, remediation typically happens outside the regular classroom—before school or at lunch or after school.

There are two types of remediation. *Short-term remediation* is designed to get students ready for the summative assessment. It is the students' final chance to reach mastery thresholds before the end of the unit. You are not reteaching the entire unit here; instead, you are focused on filling in learning gaps, reinforcing the most important concepts from the unit, and highlighting the key components of the upcoming assessment.

While short-term remediation is strictly focused on the unit at hand, *ongoing remediation* is focused on long-term skill development to address large gaps in students' background knowledge or missing foundational skills.

This chapter focuses primarily on short-term remediation. You will learn how to choose which content and skills to remediate, identify which students are most likely to reach mastery through remediation, select remediation strategies, and develop a remediation plan.

Deciding What to Remediate

Not everything students struggle with should trigger remediation. Some skills can be refined and taught in later units, and other skills might be "nice-to-knows" that are not essential for students reaching the mastery threshold. Because remediation takes some degree of time and energy from both you and students, it is important to distinguish between which content and skills absolutely need remediation and which do not.

There are two key questions that should guide your decision. First: *Will the content or skill in question make up a substantial part of the summative assessment?* If so, then remediate. If not, remediation may just serve to overwhelm students and distract them from the highest priority of information. Rather than offer remediation on every skill and concept represented in the summative assessment, choose to remediate the most important content that will give students the highest likelihood of passing.

Second: *Is the skill or content in question foundational for learning the material in the next unit or units later in the year?* If so, remediation makes sense. But if the student will not need mastery of the current concept in order to be successful in future units, simply having familiarity with the concept may be all the student needs. For instance, students may need to master the concept of tone or irony in a poetry unit because they will also need to understand these concepts in the short story and drama units later in the year. But if a student doesn't master the concept of synecdoche, she can still master the short story and drama units, given that synecdoche may not show up again in that content.

One effective way to determine what to remediate is to take a look at your summative assessment and determine which concepts constitute the largest proportion of points. These concepts are good candidates for remediation. Next, look at upcoming units and determine which concepts show up over and over again. These concepts are important for students to master and will require remediation.

Deciding Whom to Remediate

Once you have determined what content it is important to remediate, the next step is to identify which students require remediation and in what way. Start by looking at the formative assessment data you have already collected for this unit. Examine homework, classwork, and quiz results. Look at any projects, discussions, or other assignments that have informed you of students' progress toward mastery thresholds. Students who have not reached mastery thresholds for the concepts you have identified as key should receive remediation.

Next, target your remediation to specifically address each student's need. Some students may simply need a quick review of key concepts. Others will require more intensive help with specific content or skills. Rather than provide a blanket remediation strategy for all students, try to group students in order to match your approach to each student's needs. There are three groups you will want to consider when selecting remediation strategies.

Students Who Are Close to Mastery

The first group is students who are close—essentially, within a few percentage points—to a mastery threshold. These are the students who engaged with supports and interventions you provided throughout the unit and made positive progress because of your efforts. All these students require is a brief review of skills and content to prepare them for the summative assessment and make sure that their summative assessment performance will accurately reflect their learning progress.

Try to quickly remediate this group and return them to the general assessment preparation you provide for the whole class. For example, if the whole class is completing a test review packet, you might do a special session to get the targeted group started, address some of the high-incidence content and skill areas that you selected, and then let them work with classmates to complete the rest of the packet.

Students Who Need Intensive Remediation

The second group is likely to be a small one, consisting of students who have substantial skill or knowledge gaps that persist even after receiving general classroom supports and targeted interventions. They may have interacted with the interventions inconsistently, made "baby steps," or need more time to practice material.

For this group you will want to look at the areas in which they are not reaching mastery—as indicated by formative assessment data gathered during the unit—and compare these areas to your list of high-priority skills and content that will be included on the summative assessment. These students may become overwhelmed or distracted easily, so try to focus your remediation on the material that will give them the biggest "bang for the buck" on the assessment. For example, if your test on the Civil War has 10 questions about the causes of the war and only one question about a particular general, focus your remediation on the causes of the war.

Students Who Struggle More with Context Than with Content

The last group of students is a bit more difficult to identify, but remediation will probably help them make huge gains on the summative assessment. These are the students who have acquired a reasonable grasp of the unit skills and content but struggle with the test format. For example, if the test covers a unit on weather, these students have at least a fair grasp of the concepts you presented during instruction. But if you have asked students to write a paragraph explaining how tornadoes form, and you have a group of students who have demonstrated difficulty in crafting written responses, you should provide remediation on how to deconstruct a short-answer question and organize a response. Otherwise these students will not have an opportunity to effectively show you all they know about tornadoes because they will be impaired by their difficulty with written responses.

With all this in mind, use the **Remediation Grouping Worksheet** on the next page to identify and group the students who will require remediation. The best time to use this worksheet is shortly before the summative assessment in a unit.

Selecting a Remediation Strategy

To select effective remediation, you need to find out as much as you can about why a student is still struggling in the first place. In most instances, students don't need to be re-taught all of the material you have covered in a unit; it's likely they simply have

Remediation Grouping Worksheet

	Student #1	Student #2	Student #3
Student name:			
Indicator(s) that remediation is necessary:			
Interventions offered during the unit:			
Did the student engage in the interventions?	Yes Somewhat No	Yes Somewhat No	Yes Somewhat No
Did the student show progress through use of the interventions?	Yes Somewhat No	Yes Somewhat No	Yes Somewhat No
Is the student within a few percentage points of meeting mastery thresholds?	Yes Somewhat No	Yes Somewhat No	Yes Somewhat No
Does the student struggle with a particular type of assessment, rather than with content/skills? Which type?			
Remediation group:	Minimal Intensive Assessment strategies	Minimal Intensive Assessment strategies	Minimal Intensive Assessment strategies

gaps in understanding or particular misperceptions that have persisted and prevented them from grasping key concepts. When you can you pinpoint the source of a student's confusion and identify where the student got off track, you can provide the necessary course correction. Remember that when you effectively use acceleration and intervention, the number of students who will require remediation should be very small. It would be overwhelming for the teacher to remediate an entire class, but remediating two or three students is definitely manageable.

Choosing a remediation strategy is often a matter of "getting into the student's head"—of eliciting additional evidence of learning and analyzing the evidence of learning you've gathered so far. You'll need to focus on assumptions the student may be making and try to understand the logic the student is using. Questions to ask include "How did you get that answer?" "What strategy did you use here?" "Why did you select this particular strategy?" "What did you try first?" "What do you think this means?" "How did you come up with that definition?" Asking these questions will help you pinpoint the source of a student's confusion.

Another way to find out where specific students might be confused and need help is to have them summarize what they have learned, orally or in writing. As you listen to or read students' summaries, you can identify any misconceptions that persist and gain insight into what each particular student still needs to learn.

You can also look at a student's assessment data and assignments and conduct an *error analysis* to figure out why he or she is still demonstrating a lack of understanding. This is a three-step process:

1. ***Identify the key error.*** Is a student making repeated computational mistakes? Is he coming to the wrong conclusions in his essay responses? Is the student having trouble writing effective topic sentences? Is he skipping a step in a process?

2. ***Determine the key error's probable cause.*** Do computational mistakes signal that a student doesn't know a few basic math facts? Is there key information that the student isn't considering before drawing conclusions in her essay responses? Does the student understand the purpose of topic sentences and see how they relate to the thesis? Is she skipping key steps because she doesn't understand the full process?

3. ***Think about how you can help the student avoid this error in the future.*** Do you need to review math facts or review key information before the next essay? Give a student a diagram that makes clear the relationship between topic sentences and the thesis? Give a "cheat sheet" that has the steps to the process?

Once you have identified what material students still don't understand and have unpacked the key errors they are still making, you can look for remediation strategies that directly address those key errors. When you take time to uncover why a student is still confused, you can more strategically select a remediation strategy that is likely to get students back on track.

Let's take a look at some key remediation strategies.

Reteaching

In most cases, students who need remediation really need to be retaught key material. Reteaching is not simply going over the material again more slowly. It is teaching students the concepts they still don't understand *in a different way.*

Perhaps you asked students to read the material in the textbook and take notes. But even with support, some students' reading levels are so far below the textbook's reading level that they could not effectively access the content. Perhaps you taught a key concept by having students work together in groups to solve a problem, but even with support, one group of students goofed around, didn't finish the project in a meaningful way, and thus still doesn't understand the concept. Maybe you taught a key concept by having students work in learning stations, but a student was absent that day and missed a critical opportunity to have hands-on interaction with the material that would have deepened his understanding. Or maybe you have a student who is on the verge of mastery but needs additional practice outside class to cement her understanding.

All of these students need reteaching. They need another opportunity to try to learn the material—this time, in another context or through different strategies.

Reteaching can take several forms. You can meet with students outside class in small groups and go over the material in a way that is more accessible to students or at a slower pace that allows them more time to process the information. You can provide students with online support through tutorials and simulations that help them "see" a concept and interact with it in a different way. You can provide students with opportunities for additional practice they need to really understand a concept. In most cases, you are not reteaching the entire unit but just going back over key concepts, addressing learning gaps, and correcting students' errors. Now let's consider some guidelines for reteaching.

- ***Reteaching should focus on key concepts and skills.*** Rather than reteach every concept in the learning unit, focus on those concepts that are critical for students' acquisition of upcoming concepts or that will be necessary for students to pass the summative assessment.

- ***Reteaching should take place very shortly after the formative assessment.*** Don't wait until the end of the unit to offer reteaching. Try to provide reteaching as close to the original lesson as possible so that students are not asked to relearn material that has long passed while they are simultaneously trying to learn new material.

- ***Reteaching should be different from regular instruction.*** One of the primary reasons students need reteaching is that they were unable to learn the material in the original context. Thus, if you originally asked students to learn the information by reading the text, provide students with an interactive website during the reteaching session to help them learn the material in a different way. If students were originally asked to learn the material through direct instruction, offer them opportunities to work in cooperative pairs or small groups in order to relearn the material.

- ***Reteaching should not create additional work for students.*** Sometimes teachers assign remedial material that creates an additional burden for students—a review packet that must be completed on top of other homework or a Saturday remediation session that requires additional homework each week. Rather than help students, these additional assignments only serve to overwhelm them. Make reteaching a self-contained activity students can complete inside the remediation session. Do not burden students with additional work when they are already struggling to keep up.

Corrective Action and Reassessing

When formative assessment data you gather during a unit indicate that particular students need remediation, you can take a corrective action (e.g., reteach, review, or employ another of the remediation strategies addressed in this section) and follow it with a reassessment of the content in question. Although the results of students' reassessments do provide you with a way to check the effectiveness of your corrective action, having students sit for a test or quiz again or having them redo and resubmit a project or assignment is a critical component of this strategy. You are providing remediation for the content in question and also building students' "soft skills"—their ability to exhibit learning under testing conditions.

Reassessing is a controversial topic. The first point to clarify is that we are not talking about giving students a second chance at a unit summative assessment. The assessments we are talking about are the various formal and informal measures of student understanding you take *during instruction*—the tests, quizzes, and other assignments that generate formative assessment data. Still, many teachers argue that reassessment isn't fair, that it promotes laziness and gaming of the system, and that grading new sets of tests creates another burden for the teacher. It's true that when reassessment is done incorrectly, it can be all of those things. But when done correctly, reassessing is a powerful opportunity to ensure that your students reach the mastery threshold and will be able to demonstrate that they have reached it.

If you choose to reassess your students, here are the guidelines for doing it the right way:

- *Reassess only after providing some sort of reteaching or corrective action.* Students must receive some sort of reteaching or corrective action before the reassessment. Perhaps you will have them make and submit flashcards, highlight key information in their notes, redo a review guide, or rewrite a short-answer response to reflect your feedback before they are allowed to participate in a retake of the assessment. Having to participate in these learning activities helps the students who really need the retake and inconveniences the ones whose poor initial test performance was simply a result of a failure to study. Those students will soon come to see it's easier to do their best on the first attempt.

- *Reassess to improve learning, not grades.* Students need to understand that the reassessment is not about getting a higher grade but about making sure that they are learning at or above the mastery threshold. Keeping the focus on learning rather than on grades keeps students from attempting to "game the system."

- *Reassess only when it will help students learn information that they must have to move on and succeed in future units.* Otherwise, you can use a quick intervention strategy to help students improve poor performance.

- *Reassess in a new or different format, as applicable.* Unless it is important that students master a particular form of assessment in preparation for a state test, nationally normed achievement test, IB exam, or AP test, use a different kind of assessment for the retake. In this way, you keep the focus on the concepts rather than the particular learning context, and you give students a new way to demonstrate their mastery—perhaps one that is more suited to their learning preferences or skills.

- ***Reassess as close to the original assessment data as possible.*** You will require some time for reteaching or other remediation, but do your best to administer the retake before the students are immersed in the next unit. This scheduling keeps the learning from being too disjointed and helps prevent students from becoming overwhelmed.

YES, BUT...

It means a lot more work for me.

There are several ways that you can reassess students and make it manageable for you both. Instead of creating two different assessments, can you exchange assessments with another teacher in your building or district who teaches the same subject or grade level? Can you use the test associated with a different textbook? Can you give students an alternative format of the same test? Is there a CD-ROM or online resource that comes with your textbook? Many such resources have an assessments option that not only will allow students to take the assessment online but will also grade it for you and e-mail you the student's score. And instead of grading the assessments yourself, can you have your students check their answers right after they take the assessment?

Tutoring

For students who have significant gaps in their background knowledge that cannot be entirely addressed through acceleration or in-class supports, tutoring is a useful form of remediation. The key is that you don't attempt to fill *all* of the students' learning gaps; focus only on filling the gaps that are creating a significant barrier to learning.

Let's say that you are teaching students how to multiply fractions but you still have students who don't know their multiplication tables. For most students, you can simply give them practice on the multiplication tables they do know already, but for some students who don't know their tables at all, tutoring is more appropriate. You can provide this tutoring directly or have students work through an interactive online tutorial to learn the multiplication table. Or suppose your class is writing a paper and you have students who are struggling to demonstrate stylistic maturity. You can host a couple of quick tutoring sessions after school to show students how to use sentence combining strategies as a way of improving their sentence structure and style.

To ensure that you get the most out of your tutoring sessions, keep these guide-lines in mind:

- *Tutoring should focus on helping students acquire specific skills.* If students simply need generalized support, work with them during an extra help session or a homework club.

- *Tutoring should focus on helping students acquire skills that directly relate to the learning task with which they are struggling.* Part of the tutorial should be to show students how what they are learning in the tutoring session will make the learning task more doable and ultimately make them more successful.

- *Tutoring should be temporary.* Once students have learned the targeted skill, their tutoring sessions should cease.

Additional Practice

Sometimes students are stuck below a mastery threshold not because they haven't learned specific skills but because those skills are still in a fledgling state. In other words, they just need more time to practice those skills until using them becomes automatic. Practice helps students develop fluency and proficiency. When students reach automaticity, they can focus on the concept behind the process rather than on the specific steps of the process itself. Thus, additional practice is often a way to help students become better thinkers and learners.

Although practice has been used effectively as a teaching technique for as long as there's been teaching, its reputation has taken a downturn in recent years as it has become equated with "drill and kill." Used the right way, practice is an extremely powerful tool for reinforcing basic skills operations so that students are prepared to master more advanced ones. Practice provides insurance against forgetting and helps students transfer the skills they have learned to new contexts.

There are four keys to avoiding the "drill and kill" syndrome and making additional practice sessions more effective:

- *Additional practice should be distributed.* Research shows that students retain more material over a longer period of time if their practice is distributed over several practice sessions rather than crammed into one (Willingham, 2009). But practice should be distributed across activities as well as over time. Rather than use the same practice activities again and again, provide students practice within the context of more advanced skills. Yes, students can practice their multiplication tables by completing quick math drills, but they can also practice them by solving more complex problems that require them to use the same few multiplication steps repeatedly.

• ***Additional practice should be meaningful.*** Students should not practice for practice's sake. They should only be given additional practice for skills that need to become automatic so that they can get better at other, more complex skills. For instance, students should be able to identify geographic features and how they influence regions on a map of the United States, but it probably is not vital that they memorize the capital of each of the 50 states. Only provide additional practice on those skills that are prerequisite for more advanced work.

• ***Additional practice should be short.*** Part of the reason practice sessions are equated with "drilling and killing" is because they are often too long. Give students short opportunities to practice—no more than 15 minutes at a time—so that they have less chance to become bored and disengaged.

• ***Additional practice should have built-in feedback.*** Students need to know that their efforts are paying off in order to remain motivated to practice. Thus, design practice activities that give students immediate feedback so that you can reinforce even small steps toward mastery and so that they can see whether they need further work.

None of these strategies we've covered will be a magic bullet. But combined with the acceleration and intervention strategies that we have discussed, they will make your remediation efforts much more successful and give your students a strong final opportunity to learn important material before the class moves on.

Now use the **Remediation Planning Worksheet** on the next page to map out a remediation plan for your students.

Remediation Planning Worksheet

Students requiring short-term remediation

	Student #1	**Student #2**	**Student #3**
Student name:			
Summative assessment task			
Area(s) in which student is closest to meeting mastery			
Type of intervention with which student has been most successful			
Remediation strategies that match this student and assessment			
Time frame for implementation			

Students requiring long-term remediation

	Student #1	**Student #2**	**Student #3**
Student name:			
Area(s) in which student is not meeting mastery			
Key elements required for future units			
Type of intervention with which student has been most engaged			
Remediation strategies that match this student and the required elements for future units			
Time frame for implementation			
Other professionals who help to support this student			

YOUR TURN

Acquire: Examine the remediation strategies on pages 95–100 and choose one to try with your next unit of study. Pay attention to how it works and how students react to it. As you build your proficiency with the strategy, select a few others to try and reflect on.

Apply: Look back at the worksheet on page 101. Select those students in the short-term remediation group, and choose to implement one or two remediation strategies with the students in this group. Concentrate your efforts in the areas where students are closest to achieving success.

Assimilate: Look back at both groups from the worksheet on page 101. For the short-term remediation group, choose and implement a few remediation strategies. Monitor which strategies were most effective for each student in the group. For students in the long-term remediation group, identify the key skills or knowledge that they are missing that will be most important in the next unit of study. Select and implement a few remediation strategies to help those students prepare for upcoming study. Connect with other resource providers in the school who can help these students. For example, does the student work with a special educator, English language teacher, specialist, counselor, or mentor? Are there other teachers who are successfully reaching this student?

Adapt: After selecting and implementing remediation strategies for students in both the short-term and long-term remediation groups, monitor their progress. Determine which remediation techniques were most effective for each student or task. As you begin the next unit of study, find ways to incorporate these concepts into the acceleration and intervention you use for these students. Partner and share your plans with other resources in the school who also work with the student such as special educators, English language teachers, specialists, counselors, mentors, or other classroom teachers.

Ongoing Remediation

For a few students, classroom learning presents a deep and persistent challenge. These students may have identified health, emotional, or learning issues that affect them across courses and throughout their academic careers. Or these students have such deep learning gaps or holes in their educational experience that they face tremendous obstacles learning new material. Even though your interventions may be succinct and well designed, these students will not be able to maintain consistent, independent academic progress and will require long-term remediation.

Long-term remediation focuses on helping students acquire basic skills they will need to be successful not just in a particular learning unit but in multiple learning units or subject areas. Although long-term remediation may have some immediate effects on students' performance, its focus is on helping students build necessary skills over time, especially when these skills are critical to their long-term success in your course or in school in general.

As you provide long-term remediation to students, it is important to look forward as well as back. Both you and the students have limited time to catch up, so be sure to identify key skills and content that will be essential to upcoming work and to focus your attention there. For example, if your data indicate that a student does not understand basic punctuation and has missed the mark on writing a poem that uses the five senses, you must be brutally realistic about the situation and opt to spend most of your time on punctuation. It will be more useful for your student to enter the next unit or next grade level knowing how to use periods and exclamation points than for his portfolio folder to contain a poem about the five senses.

Although most of the students in your class can reach mastery thresholds with the supports you have provided before and during learning, supporting students at the end of the unit through short-term or long-term remediation gives them another chance to reach mastery thresholds and successfully finish the unit.

4

Putting It All Together

In this chapter you will . . .

- [ ] Review the steps you have learned so far.
- [ ] Develop a comprehensive progressive support plan.
- [ ] Learn how to communicate your plan to your students.
- [ ] Learn how to communicate your plan to parents.

Time-Saving Tools

You will complete work in this chapter more quickly if you have the following handy:

- [ ] The completed worksheets from Chapters 1, 2, and 3.

Now that you have spent time thinking through each of the steps to proactive support, how will you put everything together and create a comprehensive support plan for your students?

So far, you have thought through each stage in the process of providing proactive support. Now it is time to put it all together and develop a complete plan that you will use with your students.

Developing Your Plan

Let's review each of the steps involved in supporting students before, during, and after instruction.

TAKE IT STEP BY STEP

How to Support Struggling Students

1. Support students BEFORE instruction by anticipating confusion and applying acceleration strategies.
2. Support students DURING instruction by planning and delivering academic interventions in response to "red flags."
3. Support students AFTER instruction by providing remediation and review prior to your summative assessment.

Step 1: Anticipate Confusion and Apply Acceleration Strategies

The work begins with anticipating where students might be confused throughout an upcoming lesson. With that groundwork laid, you need to turn your focus to acceleration: how you will prepare students to be successful before the lesson or unit begins. This involves sharing with students your overall plan for how they will progress through the unit, teaching them strategies that will help them successfully organize their learning, activating or creating the background knowledge they will need to understand the concepts in the unit, and pre-exposing them to key vocabulary. The purpose behind all these strategies? To help students' learning be more productive and to prevent most students from falling into destructive struggle.

Step 2: Plan and Deliver Interventions in Response to "Red Flags"

All teachers must be prepared to address the reality of students who, despite the application of acceleration strategies, still encounter destructive struggle during the unit and require progressive intervention. Here, you set your mastery thresholds, establish the "red flags" that signal when students are headed for destructive struggle, and determine which interventions you will use to help students quickly get back on track. You also monitor the effectiveness of your interventions and decide how to gradually scale back your support as students improve or how to intensify your interventions should students fail to demonstrate improvement.

Step 3: Provide Remediation and Review Before Your Summative Assessment

With the end of a unit or a summative assessment approaching, the small number of students who have not responded to intervention require remediation to help them fill in persistent learning gaps. The work here involves selecting reteaching and re-assessment strategies that can help students who still struggle and providing students with additional support through tutoring and additional practice opportunities. As you help these students firm up shaky understanding of key concepts, you prepare them to be successful in future units.

The **Proactive Support Plan Template** on the next two pages will help you turn the information you have captured in this guide's worksheets into a comprehensive, proactive support plan for a specific unit you teach.

Proactive Support Plan Template

Unit Title:	
Key Concept:	
Mastery Thresholds:	
Supporting Students Before Instruction	
Activating Strategy: (See the list of strategies on page 26.)	
Vocabulary Strategy: (Use the worksheet on pages 40–41.)	
Organizing Strategy: (Use the worksheet on page 35.)	

Proactive Support Plan Template (cont.)

Supporting Students During Instruction	
Teaching Strategies:	
"Red Flags": (Use the worksheet on page 65.)	
Interventions: (Use the worksheet on page 81.)	
Supporting Students After Instruction	
Remediation Grouping Strategy: (Use the worksheet on page 93.)	
Remediation Planning Strategy: (Use the worksheet on page 101.)	

Communicating Your Plan to Students

It is important that students understand that the purpose of your proactive support plan is to do everything within your power to ensure their success in your course. At the very beginning of the school year, publish your plan in your class newsletter, post it on your class website, or publish it in your course syllabus. You can even post it in the classroom. Write it in "kid-friendly" language and explain your support plan to students.

Your explanation of the plan is critical. Help students understand that the plan's purpose is to ensure they will succeed. If their performance triggers a red flag, they are not in trouble; it simply means they need additional support. And be sure to stress that needing extra support does not mean they are "dumb"; it means that the current strategies they are using are not working to help them learn. Show students how the supports can get them back on track, and clarify that they can exit the plan as soon as they *do* get back on track.

Students need to know that the proactive support plan is automatic; it doesn't single out certain students. Make it clear to them that any student who triggers a red flag automatically gets additional support and will continue to receive that support *until he or she is successful.*

Additionally, show students how the plan creates shared responsibility. Point out that the plan will ask the students to do things to get back on track but also requires certain things from the teacher as well. That way, students can see how you are also invested in their success. If students can understand how the plan is designed to help them, they will be much more willing to cooperate with you as you implement the plan. **Appendix A** shows an example of how to communicate the basics of a proactive support plan to elementary, middle, and high school students.

Communicating Your Plan to Parents

If you want to enlist parents as partners, it is important that they understand how your proactive support plan works. Outline your plan in a letter you send home at the beginning of the school year. You might even create a contract that parents can sign promising to reinforce the plan at home.

If your school has a "Back to School" night, spend most of your time explaining the plan to parents and showing them how the plan is designed to help their children.

Talk about "red flags" and what they signal so parents will grasp that their children will not be singled out or placed on a lower track as a result of triggering a red flag. *All* students who trigger a red flag automatically receive support no matter who they are.

Be sure to point out that the support plan is not a remedial program. Otherwise, many parents could draw the false conclusion that your supports are only designed for students who are failing. Instead, highlight the preventive nature of the plan and show them how it will keep their children from failing. Doing so will make it much more likely that parents will support your plan during the school year. See **Appendix B** for a sample letter home to parents.

Advice for Coteachers

Developing a comprehensive support plan can also be a great way to negotiate co-teaching relationships. Both the subject-area teacher and the special educator can create a plan that gives all the students in a full-inclusion classroom the supports they need.

Because the supports in your plan will be available to all students, coteachers can apply them without singling out those students who have been identified as needing additional support and services. The supports are a part of the classroom structure, and any student can access them.

If you are teaching in a cotaught classroom, here are some guidelines for developing and implementing a comprehensive support plan:

- As you and your coteacher meet to plan lessons, spend some time anticipating areas of confusion. Use these potential areas as starting points for determining what adjusted materials and additional supports students will need and who will be responsible for providing these supports.

- Determine whether all students need the same degree of acceleration. Students with special needs often need more acceleration than other students. One teacher can provide these students with additional acceleration while the other teacher leads the class in an activating strategy.

- Using graphic organizers and cheat sheets for students with special needs is a great way to provide them with alternative materials. Instead of giving these students an "easier" worksheet to complete, give them the same worksheet but embedded with clues and tools that will allow them to complete it successfully. Not only does this cut down on the amount of work you have to do, it also cuts down on the stigma associated with getting a different worksheet.

- If the special education students have a study hall or learning skills class in addition to the regular course, spend the time in those classes accelerating grade-level content rather than remediating and reteaching. Starting a week before the lesson or unit, preview upcoming material and give these students extra strategies they can use to access the lesson more effectively and keep up with the rest of the class.

- During instruction, as one teacher is teaching, the other can be circulating, reviewing students' work, and looking for red flags. The moment the second teacher notices a red flag, that teacher can intervene on the spot or wait until students are working to provide additional help to those students who have triggered the red flag.

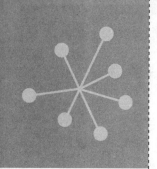

Conclusion

Supporting struggling students is not a haphazard process. It requires you to carefully think through your objectives, anticipate where students are most likely to have difficulty, and put structures in place to prevent as much confusion as possible. It means preparing supports ahead of time so that you are ready to shore up students the moment they begin to slip and can quickly get them back on track. It means having a plan for students who continue to struggle to ensure that they consistently get the assistance they need before, during, and after the lesson and can make progress toward mastery over time.

As you develop your own proactive support plan, here are a few final tips to keep in mind:

- *Effective support is repeated.* Remember, struggling students need repeated exposures to strategies in order to use these strategies automatically. Just because you have taught a strategy once does not mean that students will spontaneously make that strategy a part of their repertoire. Only when students have the opportunity to use a strategy repeatedly will they learn to benefit from it.

- *Effective support is focused.* The supports you select cannot merely address general educational concerns; they must target the specific learning challenges that are preventing students from reaching the mastery threshold.

- *Effective support is systematic.* Making support strategies a part of the structure of your classroom makes it more likely that all students can get the help they need when they need it.

- ***Effective support is temporary.*** Supports are most effective when they are temporary and gradually removed as students develop their own skills and expand their own background knowledge. Be careful not to confuse the supports with the instruction itself. Supports are designed to help students access instruction; support should not be the primary instructional strategy.

- ***Effective support provides clear directions.*** When students struggle, they need clarity more than ever. They need you to demystify the process of learning. Give them step-by-step directions that explain exactly what they need to do to successfully complete a learning activity.

- ***Effective support keeps the big picture central to students.*** Sometimes students and teachers get so caught up in lesson processes that they miss the bigger picture. They forget what they are supposed to be learning, or they don't understand how what they are doing will help them achieve mastery. Design your supports to help students make connections between the various parts of the unit and develop a more comprehensive understanding of the key concepts. This is a way to prevent students from getting bogged down by the details and concentrate instead on the purpose of their work.

- ***Effective support makes the path to mastery clear.*** The best supports not only provide students with models, examples, and clear rubrics that convey what mastery looks like, but also provide examples and models of how to achieve mastery. Showing students how to progress down this path reduces their uncertainty and disappointment and makes the goal of mastery seem more achievable.

- ***Effective support is progressive.*** Rather than overwhelm students with an intensive support or intervention every time they face difficulty, provide them with the least amount of support they need to reach mastery on their own. If minimal support does not work, however, it is important to have other, more intensive supports available. The objective is to ensure that students receive the right amount of support for them.

The right support measures, planned and in place before students show signs of failure, help prevent failure in the first place. If we carefully monitor students so that we can intervene the moment they begin to flounder, and if we provide several opportunities for our students to be successful, not only will our students thrive but many more of them would meet or exceed the standards.

But effective support practices are for teachers as well as our students. How many times have you been frustrated when students, despite your best efforts, just don't get it? How many times have you felt trapped in a remediation cycle because your students aren't keeping up with the pacing of your curriculum? Developing proactive supports is a way to mitigate these frustrations—and even prevent them. You can feel more confident that your efforts will pay off because you have spent the time carefully mapping out how you will help all of your students succeed.

As we come to the end of this how-to guide, keep in mind that learning is a continuous process. Going through this guide once will not make you a master at supporting your students. You will need to revisit the process outlined here again and again, each time refining your skill set and growing in your own ability to seamlessly *apply, assimilate*, and, ultimately, *adapt* what you learn. But doing so will yield rich rewards for both you and your students.

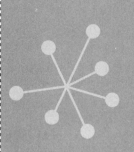

Appendixes

Appendix A Sample Proactive Support Plans
Elementary School Example

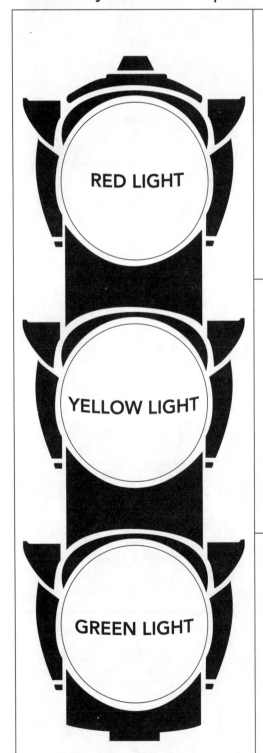

- When the teacher showed us something new, I got lost or behind.
- When we talked about what we were learning, I couldn't explain what I know.
- When the teacher gave a new assignment, I didn't know how to get started.
- When I tried my homework, it was hard to figure out and I couldn't do it.
- When we took a test or a quiz, I got many answers wrong.
- During class, I feel confused, frustrated, or lost a lot of the time.

When your work is in the Red Light Zone, your teacher will spend extra time with you or show you how to do things again or in a different way so your work gets stronger.

- When the teacher showed us something new, I got a little lost or behind.
- When we talked about what we were learning, I could explain a little bit of what I know.
- When the teacher gave a new assignment, I wasn't sure how to get started.
- When I tried my homework, it was hard to figure out what to do or I could only do part of it.
- When we took a test or a quiz, I didn't get as many answers right as I could have.
- During class, I sometimes feel confused, frustrated, or lost.

When your work is in the Yellow Light Zone, your teacher will spend extra time with you so that your work gets stronger.

- When the teacher showed us something new, I could keep up.
- When we talked about what we were learning, I could explain what I know.
- When the teacher gave a new assignment, I could get started right away.
- When I tried my homework, I understood what to do and could finish it.
- When we took a test or a quiz, I got almost everything right.
- During class, I didn't feel confused, frustrated, or lost.

When your work is in the Green Light Zone, keep working! Your teacher is always here to provide help if you need it.

Middle School Example

Dear Students,

I am excited about the year we are going to spend together learning. In order to make sure that you learn as much as possible and that you have a great experience this year, I want to make sure that we all know and do our jobs.

Your Job as a Student	My Job as Your Teacher
Come to each new unit ready to learn.	Remind you of what you know already to help you be ready for the unit and show you how what you know will help you learn something new.
Become a better learner.	Provide you with strategies you need to become a better learner.
Try to understand what you are learning.	Teach you the vocabulary you need to understand what we are doing.
Try to make connections between what we are doing in class and what you are supposed to be learning.	Provide you with learning maps that explain how what we are doing connects to what we are supposed to be learning.
Use effective strategies that will help you learn and remember what you are learning.	Show you effective strategies to help you learn and remember what you are learning.
Ask for help when you need it.	Watch you closely to see when you need help and then give you the help you need to get back on track.
Work hard to understand the concepts in the unit.	Find several different ways to explain things so that you understand.
Practice so that your work gets better.	Provide you with opportunities to practice and strategies that will make your practice more effective.
Show that you have learned what you were supposed to have learned.	Give you several different chances to show what you know, and when you show that you haven't learned something yet, give you another chance to learn it.
Work with the teacher to relearn the things that you don't get the first time.	Help you figure out what you don't know yet and reteach you or give you other ways to learn it.

Sometimes this year, even when you have done your job, you may meet with difficulty. Because I want you to learn as much as you can and have a good time doing it, I have set up some early warning signals that let me know when you need extra help and support. When you trigger an early warning, I will immediately give you the extra help you need to get back on track. Once you are back on track, you will no longer need my help and can do things on your own.

Early Warning Signal	**Support**
If you earn a D or F on a test or quiz . . .	I will spend time helping you learn the material and give you another chance to take the test or quiz.
If you get more than four problems wrong on your homework . . .	I will write a pass for you to attend homework club, where you can get extra help.
If you show that you do not understand something in class . . .	I will take time to meet with you in a small group and re-explain the material.
If you miss a checkpoint on an important assignment or show that you are headed in the wrong direction . . .	I will provide materials or meet with you to get you back on track.
If you don't turn in work when it is due . . .	I will meet with you to figure out why the work was not turned in and make a plan for how to complete the assignments.
If you can't figure out assignments in class or at home . . .	I will help you learn strategies to understand the directions and get started on your own.

High School Example: Sample Syllabus Entry

Extra Support

Because I am invested in your success this year, I am committed to doing everything I can to help you. Thus, I have set up a system to get you the help you need the moment you need it. That way, if you begin to struggle, you can quickly get back on track.

I will help you get ready to learn by

- Using learning maps at the start of each new unit so that you can see how all the parts of the unit fit together.
- Giving you strategies that will help you be successful throughout the unit.
- Explaining the vocabulary in a way that will help you understand it.
- Connecting what you are about to learn with what you know already. That way, you will be less confused and can see how all that we learn this year fits together.

I will help you be more efficient learners by

- Teaching you effective strategies that will help you get better at learning.
- Showing you how to ask for help when you need it.
- Checking your progress regularly to make sure that you are keeping up.
- Providing you with extra support when you struggle.
- Giving you regular feedback that shows you how close you are coming to meeting or exceeding the objectives of the unit.

I will help you when you encounter difficulty by

- Giving you opportunities to retake an assessment when your assessment performance reveals that there is still information you need to learn.
- Providing you with additional resources to help you learn more effectively.
- Giving you extra help when you don't understand something.
- Teaching you additional strategies you can use when the strategies you are using are not proving effective.
- Giving you opportunities to relearn material that you have demonstrated you have not learned completely.
- Showing you how to monitor your own progress so that you can ask for and get the help you need.

Because everyone needs help sometimes, these supports are available to every student in this class, regardless of your grades. And because you may not always be able to tell right away that you need extra help, I have developed some "red flags" that help me keep track of where you are and get you the support you need right away. The moment you trigger a red flag, I have supports in place that will get you back on track as quickly as possible.

Here are some red flags we will use this year:

Red Flag	Support
GPA 74% or below at the 2-week checkpoint	Conference and work audit to see where the problem might be. Together we will develop a support plan.
GPA 74% or below at interim time	Conference with your parents. Mandatory lunchtime work sessions twice per week.
GPA 74% or below at the 6-week checkpoint	Possible interventions include • Mandatory test retakes • Peer tutoring • Extra acceleration • Mandatory catch-up sessions for missed work
Test grade of 69% or below	Mandatory test-prep online tutorial and retake
Paper grade of *D* or *F*	Mandatory error analysis and rewrite

Appendix B Sample Parent Support Contract

Dear Parents or Guardians:

I am so excited to be your child's teacher this year. I am committed to making sure that your child has a great experience in my class and becomes a better learner. In order to make sure that your child reaches the goals of the course, I have set up a support plan designed to give your child the support he or she needs as soon as he or she needs it.

I have also committed to doing a number of things to set your child up for success. At the beginning of each unit, I will give your child a learning map that will help him or her understand what we are about to learn and how it connects to what we have learned already. I will also give your child a few strategies that he or she can use to organize the unit content. This will help your child make connections and learn more effectively. And I will focus on helping your child understand the key vocabulary of the unit so that he or she will be ready to learn. I will send the vocabulary home with your child and post it on the class website. Please take some time to go over this vocabulary at home with your child.

During each unit, I will monitor your child's progress to make sure that he or she is learning effectively. While some struggle in learning is to be expected, I want to make sure that your child knows how to work his or her way out of struggle. In the attached chart, I have listed the signals your child might give me to let me know that he or she needs extra help and the supports I already have in place to quickly get your child the help that's needed. I would encourage you to look for these signals as you work with your child at home and contact me directly should you see them. That way, we can work together to get your child the support he or she needs as soon as possible.

As your child receives support and starts to demonstrate success, I will gradually withdraw these supports so that your child can learn to be successful on his or her own. In the event that the provided supports don't seem to be working, I have additional supports at the ready and will continue to work with your child until he or she is successful.

Here is where I need your help. Some of these supports require that you review material with your child at home. Some of them may involve your child staying after school, meaning you will need to arrange for transportation home when the support session is over. However, the most important way you can support your child is by staying in touch with me and letting me know if you notice that your child needs additional support based on the "red flags" above. Together, we can make sure that your child has a successful year in my class.

_____   _____
Teacher Signature   Date   Parent/Guardian Signature   Date

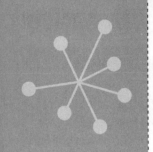

References

Buffum, A., Mattos, M., & Weber, C. (2009). *Pyramid response to intervention: RTI, professional learning communities, and how to respond when kids don't learn.* Bloomington, IN: Solution Tree.

Dweck, C. (2006). *Mindset: The new psychology of success.* New York: Random House.

Jackson, R. R. (2009). *Never work harder than your students and other principles of great teaching.* Alexandria, VA: ASCD.

Marzano, R. J. (2003). Direct vocabulary instruction: An idea whose time has come. In B. William (Ed.), *Closing the achievement gap: A vision for changing beliefs and practices* (2nd ed., pp. 48–66). Alexandria, VA: ASCD.

Marzano, R. J., Pickering, D. J., & Pollock, J. E. (2001). *Classroom instruction that works: Research-based strategies for increasing student achievement.* Alexandria, VA: ASCD.

Thompson, M., Thompson, J., & Thompson, S. (2005). *Catching kids up: Learning-focused strategies for acceleration.* Boone, NC: Learning Concepts, Inc.

Willingham, D. T. (2009). *Why don't students like school? A cognitive scientist answers questions about how the mind works and what it means for the classroom.* San Francisco: Jossey-Bass.

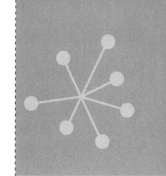

About the Authors

Robyn R. Jackson, PhD, is a former high school teacher and middle school administrator. She is currently the President and Founder of Mindsteps Inc., a professional development firm for teachers and administrators that provides workshops and materials designed to help any teacher reach every student. Dr. Jackson is the author of *Never Work Harder Than Your Students and Other Principles of Great Teaching*, *The Differentiation Workbook,* and *The Instructional Leader's Guide to Strategic Conversations with Teachers* as well as the how-to guides in the **Mastering the Principles of Great Teaching** series. You can sign up for Dr. Jackson's monthly e-newsletter at www.mindstepsinc.com, follow Dr. Jackson on Twitter at @robyn_mindsteps, or reach her via e-mail at robyn@mindstepsinc.com.

Claire Lambert has taught middle school English and reading and has worked to support teachers as a school-based staff developer. She is currently an independent consultant with Mindsteps Inc., and the instructor for a variety of online professional development courses for teachers. Ms. Lambert also is a regular contributor to the Mindsteps blog. You can contact her at claire@mindstepsinc.com and read more of her work at www.mindsteps incblog.com.

Want More?

Additional resources are available on this book's companion website at www.mindstepsinc.com/support. There, you can

- Download copies of the worksheets in this book.
- Find and link to additional free resources.
- Download related video content that provides additional explanations.
- Post your own comments and hear what other readers are saying.
- Sign up to receive a free monthly e-newsletter.
- Explore lots of other reader-only content.

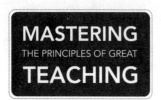

Watch for other books in this series, coming soon.

 Much more about master teachers can be found in this series' companion book, *Never Work Harder Than Your Students and Other Principles of Great Teaching* by Robyn R. Jackson (#109001).